U0511408

A Midsummer
Night's Dream

··❦··莎翁戏剧经典 ··❦··

仲夏夜之梦

〔英〕威廉·莎士比亚 著

裴克安 注释

商务印书馆
SINCE 1897
The Commercial Press

2016 年·北京

威廉·莎士比亚

图 1

图 2（见 4 页）

Athens. The Palace of THESEUS.

Enter THESEUS, HIPPOLYTA, PHILOSTRATE, *and*
  ATTENDATS.]

THESEUS. Now, fair Hippolyta, our nuptial hour
  Draws on apace; four happy days bring in
  Another moon.

图 3（见 20—22 页）

The same. QUINCE'S *house.*

Enter QUINCE, SNOUT, BOTTOM, FLUTE, SNOUT，and STARVE-
    LING.]

QUINCE. Is all our company here?

BOTTOM. You were best to call them generally, man
    by man, according to the scrip.

QUINCE. Here is the scroll of every man's name,
    which is thought fit, through all Athens, to play
    in our interlude before the duke and the duchess,
    on his wedding-day at night.

图 4 (见 28 页)

QUINCE. At the duke's oak we meet.
BOTTOM. Enough; hold or cut bow-strings.

图 5（见 30 页）

PUCK. How now, spirit! whither wander you?
FAIRY. Over hill, over dale,

    Thorough bush, thorough brier,

Over park, over pale,

    Thorough flood, thorough fire,

I do wander everywhere.

图 6（见 34 页）

OBERON. Tarry, rash wanton: am not I thy lord?
TITANIA. Then I must be thy lady: but I know
　　When thou hast stolen away from fairy land,
　　And in the shape of Corin sat all day,
　　Playing on pipes of corn, and versing love
　　To amorous Phillida.

图 7（见 36 页）

TITANIA. Set your heart at rest:
    The fairy land buys not the child of me.

图 **8**（见 38 页）

OBERON.　How long within this wood intend you stay?

图 9（见 40 页）

OBERON. That very time I saw, but thou couldest not,
  Flying between the cold moon and the earth,
  Cupid all arm'd: a certain aim he took
  At a fair vestal throned by the west,
  And loosed his love-shaft smartly from his bow,
  As it should pierce a hundred thousand hearts.

图 10（见 48 页）

FIRST FAIRY. You spotted snakes with double tongue，
   Thorny hedgehogs，be not seen；
  Newts and blind-worms，do no wrong，
   Come not near our fairy queen.
   CHORUS.
  Philomel，with melody，
  Sing in our sweet lullaby；
Lulla，lulla，lullaby，lulla，lulla，lullaby.

图 11（见 58 页）

BOTTOM. Are we all met?

QUINCE. Pat，pat；and here's a marvelous convenient
  place for our rehearsal.

图 **12**（见 60 页）

SNOUT. Will not the ladies be afeard of the lion?

...

BOTTOM. Masters，you ought to consider with yourselves：to bring in，— God shield us!

图 13（见 66 页）

BOTTOM. I see their knavery: this is to make an ass of me; to fright me, if they could. But I will not stir from this place, do what they can: I will walk up and down here, and I will sing, that they shall hear I am not afraid. [*Sings*.

> The ousel cock so black of hue,
>> With orange-tawny bill,
> The throstle with his note so true,
>> The wren with little quill.

图 14（见 70 页）

OBERON. I wonder if Titania be awaked;
　　Then, what it was that next came in her eye,
　　Which she must dote on in extremity.

图 15（见 72 页）

PUCK. When they him spy,
　　　As wild geese that the creeping fowler eye,
　　　Or russet-pated choughs, many in sort,
　　　Rising and cawing at the gun's report,
　　　Sever themselves and madly sweep the sky,
　　　So, at his sight, away his fellows fly.

图 16（见 98 页）

DEMETRIUS.   Yea, art thou there?

PUCK. Follow my voice：we'll try no manhood here.

图 17（见 104 页）

TITANIA. Come，sit thee down upon this flowery bed，
    While I thy amiable cheeks do coy，
And stick musk-roses in thy sleek smooth head，
    And kiss thy fair large ears，my gentle joy.

图 18（见 106 页）

BOTTOM. I have a reasonable good ear in music. Let's have the tongs and the bones.

图 19(见 122—124 页)

HIPPOLYTA. But all the story of the night told over，
  And all their minds transfigured so together，
  More witnesseth than fancy's images，
  And grows to something of great constancy；
  But，howsoever，strange and admirable.

THESEUS. Here come the lovers，full of joy and mirth.

"莎翁戏剧经典"丛书总序

　　莎士比亚(William Shakespeare，1564—1616)是英国16世纪文艺复兴时期的伟大剧作家和诗人，也是世界文坛上的巨擘。他一生创作了38部戏剧作品(一说37部)，诗作包括两部长篇叙事诗、一部十四行诗集以及其他一些短篇诗作。四百多年来这些作品被翻译成多种文字，在世界各地广泛传播。正如他同时代的批评家和剧作家本·琼生所说，他是"时代的灵魂"，"不属一个时代，而属于所有的时代！"莎士比亚在世期间，他的戏剧作品曾吸引了大量观众，包括宫廷王室成员和普通百姓，产生了巨大影响。18世纪以来，这些作品始终活跃在舞台上，20世纪随着电影业的发展，它们又被搬上银幕。几百年来，无论是体现莎士比亚原作的表演还是经过不断改编的作品，莎剧都拥有众多的观者，散发出不灭的艺术光辉；另一方面，自1623年莎士比亚全集第一对开本问世，莎士比亚的戏剧也成为学者和广大普通读者阅读、学习、研究的对象，在历代读者的阅读和研究中，这些作品不断得到新阐释和挖掘。莎士比亚的作品焕发着永久不衰的生命活力。

　　1564年4月，莎士比亚出生于英格兰中部的埃文河畔的斯特拉福镇。家境殷实，父亲曾经营手套和羊毛，并做过小镇的镇长。莎士比亚小时曾在镇上的文法学校读书，受到过较为正规的拉丁文和古典文学的教育。不久，家道中落，陷入经济困境，这可能成为莎士比亚后来未能进入大学读书的原因。1582年，莎士比亚十八岁时与邻村一位大他八岁的女子安·哈撒韦成婚，六个月后，大女儿苏珊娜降生，此后他们又有了一对孪生子女，不幸的是，儿子哈姆内特早夭。16世纪90年代左右，莎士比亚来到伦敦，发展他的戏剧事业。他曾是剧团的演员、编剧和股东。90年代初期，莎士比亚即开始戏剧创作。1592年，莎士比亚已在同行中崭露头角,被当时的"大学才子"剧作家格林所嫉妒,他把莎士比亚称作"那只新抖起来的乌鸦","借我们的羽毛来打扮自己……狂妄地幻想着能独自震撼(Shake-scene)这个国家的舞台"。1592—1594年间,伦敦因流行瘟疫,大部分剧院关闭,在此期间莎士比亚完成了两部著名的长篇叙事诗《维纳斯与阿多尼斯》与《鲁克丽丝受辱记》。1594年剧院恢复营业之后,莎士比亚加入宫廷大臣剧团,并终生服务于该剧团,直到1613年离开伦敦返回家乡。90年代中期,他进入了戏剧创作的巅峰时期。在1590年至1613年的二十多年之间,莎士比亚共创作了历史剧、悲剧、喜剧、传奇剧等38部。90年代中后期,他的创作以喜剧和历史剧为主,包括喜剧《仲夏夜之梦》(1595)、《威尼斯商人》(1596)、《无事生非》(1598—1599)、《皆大欢喜》(1599—1600)等和大部分历史剧,如《理查三世》(1592—1593)、《亨利四世》(上、下)(1596—1598)、《亨利五世》(1598—1599)等。这一时期,他的创作风格较为明快,充满积极向上的格调,即便剧中有悲剧的成分,整个作品也透露出对生活的肯定,对理想的向往,如《罗密欧与朱丽叶》(1595)。进入17世纪后,莎士比亚的戏剧更多地转向对人生重大问题的思考,探索解决人生之困顿的途径,诸如权力、欲望、嫉妒、暴政等等。四大悲剧《哈姆莱特》(1600—1601)、《奥瑟罗》(1603—1604)、《李尔王》(1605—1606)、《麦克白》(1606)均完成于这一时期。此外,几部重要的罗马题材剧也在90年代末和新世纪的最初几年完成,如《裘力·凯撒》(1599)、《安东尼与克里奥佩特拉》(1606)、《科里奥兰纳斯》(1608)等。莎士比亚这一时期也创作了几部喜剧,但风格较前一时期更多悲情色彩,更为沉重而引人深思。1609年,莎士比亚《十四行诗集》出版。晚期的莎士比亚剧作风格有一定变化,最有影响的是传奇剧,如《暴风雨》,通过想象的世界与现实世界的对照来探讨人生问题。

莎士比亚的名字开始传入中国是在19世纪中上叶,他的戏剧被翻译成汉语而为国人所知则是在20世纪初期。当时,他剧作的内容通过英国19世纪兰姆姐弟《莎士比亚戏剧故事集》的汉译被介绍到中国来，即无译者署名的《澥外奇谭》(1903)和林纾、魏易翻译的《吟边燕语》(1904)。20世纪20年代，莎剧汉译事业的开拓者田汉翻了《哈孟雷特》(1921)和《罗密欧与朱丽叶》(1924)。此后，朱生豪、梁实秋、孙大雨、曹禺、曹未风、虞尔昌等译家都翻译过莎士比亚的剧作。朱生豪先生在经历日本侵略的苦难、贫穷和疾病折磨的极其艰苦的环境下，以惊人的毅力和顽强的意志，克服种种艰难险阻，穷毕生之精力完成了31部半莎剧的翻译，成为播撒莎士比亚文明之火的普罗米修斯，译莎事业的英雄和圣徒。他的莎剧译文优美畅达，人物性格鲜明，成为广大读者所珍爱的艺术瑰宝。梁实秋是中国迄今为止唯一一位个人独立完成莎剧和莎诗汉译工程的翻译家。梁译有详尽的注释和说明，学术含量较高。1956年，卞之琳翻译的《哈姆雷特》出版，他完善了孙大雨提出的翻译原则，提出"以顿代步、韵式依原诗、等行翻译"的翻译方法，可谓开一代诗体译法之风，他的译本至今都被视作该剧最优秀的译本。方平是另一位重要的成绩卓著的莎剧翻译家。2000年由他主编主译的《新莎士比亚全集》出版，其中25部莎剧由方平翻译，其他作品由阮坤、吴兴华、汪义群、覃学岚、屠岸、张冲等译出，为国内目前首部全部由分行诗体翻译的莎剧莎诗全集。

时至今日，莎士比亚的戏剧作品仍不断有新的译本出版，对广大读者而言，阅读汉译的莎剧已经是一件十分方便的事情，而这些汉译莎剧作品中不乏优秀的译本。然而，尽管莎剧的汉译丰富多彩，莎剧的改编层出不穷，要想真正了解莎剧的本来面目，我们还需要回到莎剧原文本身。其中的原因有三：一、每一种语言都是丰富的，其表达的意义可能是多元多面的，但由于译出语和译入语两种语言之间的差异，再好的翻译也只能尽可能地贴近原文而不可能百分之百地再现原文的魅力，因此，阅读再好的译本也无法取代或等同于阅读原作；二、莎士比亚生活的时代距今已经有约400年，他所使用的英语与今天人们所熟悉的英语已有较大差异，当时的人们所熟悉的文化和历史事件也是我们今天并不熟知的，因此，要真正领悟他的作品，还须回到他那时的语言和文化中去;三、莎剧经过约 400 年的变迁,在改编中不断变换,有些已经走出了莎士比亚时代的莎剧,因而,想要认识和了解莎剧,最佳的办法还是回到莎剧的原文本中去。

莎士比亚生活和创作的时期在 16 世纪末 17 世纪初。英语在当时已经得到极大的发展,十分活跃而成熟,尤其莎士比亚戏剧中所运用的英语,文辞丰富、结构灵活、表达力很强。但随着时代的发展,其中的一些用词、用语以及语义等都发生了变化,与我们今天的英语存在一定距离,理解起来也就会有一定困难。莎剧在绝大多数情况下采用的是诗体写作,即人物的语言是分行的,每行十个音节,轻重音节相间,一轻一重的每两个音节构成一个音步,不押韵,因此,他的剧作均为抑扬格五音步的素体诗。这样的诗体形式突显出莎剧语言的艺术魅力,音韵优美、铿锵,节奏感强,表达生动有力。然而,正因为这是诗体写作,在语法上就可能出现诗语言特有的结构,比如倒装句或词序颠倒的现象等。莎剧的语言丰富多彩,不同人物的话语呈现出多种特色,时而体现出古典拉丁语的文风,时而出现双关语、俚语、隐喻等修辞手法。典故、历史事件、政治元素、宗教、生活习俗等等都可能成为今天的读者理解莎剧原文本的障碍。因而,借助良好的注释来理解莎剧的原作就成为我们了解和认识莎剧原貌的必要手段。这次由商务印书馆隆重推出的"莎翁戏剧经典"丛书,重点选出莎士比亚的 12 部经典剧作,在裘克安先生主编的"莎士比亚注释"丛书的基础上进行了改编修订,并加入了精美的插图。裘先生主编的"莎士比亚注释"丛书对莎剧原文做了多方面的详尽注释,对理解原文起到有效作用,在读者中有较广泛的影响。相信这套"莎翁戏剧经典"的出版会进一步推动莎剧在广大读者中的影响力,提高人们对阅读莎剧以及经典文学作品原文的兴趣和能力,产生积极的和广泛的影响。

屠岸 章燕

2013 年 10 月 4 日

"莎士比亚注释"丛书总序

　　莎士比亚研究在新中国有过不平坦的道路和坎坷的命运。解放后不久,大家纷纷学俄语,学英语的人数骤减。研究英国文学,要看苏联人怎么说。"文革"十年,莎士比亚同其他西方"资产阶级"作家一样被打入冷宫。改革开放以后,1978年人民文学出版社出版了在朱生豪译文基础上修订补足的《莎士比亚全集》。随之又出版了一些个别剧的不同译本,如方平译的《莎士比亚喜剧五种》(1979年)和卞之琳译的《莎士比亚悲剧四种》(1988年)。梁实秋的译本,现在大陆上也可以读到了。评介和研究莎士比亚的文章,从"文革"结束后才逐渐多起来。

　　但是,目前多数人学习、欣赏和研究莎士比亚,是通过中译文来进行的。精通英语而研究莎士比亚的学者不是没有,然而他们人数不多,年纪却老迈了。最近若干年,才有一些年轻人到英国或美国去学习和研究莎士比亚。

　　1981年我就想到有必要在中国出版我们自己注释的莎士比亚著作。谈起来,许多朋友都赞成。1984年中国莎士比亚研究会筹备和成立时,我自告奋勇,联系了一些志同道合的学者,共同开始编写莎士比亚注释本。商务印书馆大力支持出版这套丛书。到2002年底已出书26种,而且第一次印刷版已全部售完。这证明这套丛书是很受欢迎的。

　　要知道,莎士比亚是英语文学中最优秀的代表人物,他又是英语语言大师,学习、欣赏和研究他的原著,是译文无法替代的。商务印书馆以其远见卓识,早在1910年和1921—1935年间,就出版过几种莎士比亚剧本的注释本,以满足这方面的需求。那时的教会学校学生英文水平高,能读莎著;不但大学生能读,连有些中学生都能读。可从那时以后,整整50年中国就没印过原文的莎士比亚著作。

世界各国，莎著的注释本多得不计其数。如果唯独中国没有，实在说不过去。如果没有，对于中国知识分子欣赏和研究莎士比亚十分不利。近年来，中国人学英语的越来越多了，他们的英文水平也逐渐提高了。因此，也存在着一定的读者市场。

有了注释本，可以为明天的莎士比亚研究提供一个可靠的群众基础。而译本显然不能提供可靠的基础。

莎士比亚是 16、17 世纪之交的作者，他写的又是诗剧。对于现代的读者，他的英语呈现着不少的困难。不要说掌握了现代英语的中国读者，就是受过一般教育的英美人士，在初读莎士比亚原著时也面临许多障碍，需要注释的帮助。

莎士比亚的时代，英语正从受屈折变化拘束的中世纪英语，向灵活而丰富的现代英语转变。拉丁语和法语当时对英语影响很大。而莎士比亚对英语的运用又有许多革新和创造。主要的困难可以归纳为以下几个方面，也就是注释要提供帮助的方面：

（一）词汇。许多词虽然拼法和现在一样，但具有不同的早期含义，不能望文生义。另有一些词拼法和现在不一样，而含义却相同。莎士比亚独创了一些词。他特别喜欢用双关语，在他创作的早期尤其如此。而双关语是无从翻译的。这是译本无论如何也代替不了注释本的原因之一。

让我们举《哈姆莱特》剧中男主角出场后最初讲的几句话为例：

> King：But now，my cousin Hamlet，and my son —
> Hamlet〔Aside〕：A little more than kin，and less than kind！
> King：How is it that the clouds still hang on you？
> Hamlet：Not so，my lord．I am too much i' the sun．

• 梁实秋的译文如下：

> 王：现在，我的侄子哈姆雷特，也是我的儿子，——
> 哈〔旁白〕：比侄子是亲些，可是还算不得儿子。
> 王：怎么，你脸上还是罩着一层愁云？
> 哈：不是的，陛下；我受的阳光太多了。

• 卞之琳的译文如下：

王：得，哈姆雷特，我的侄子，我的儿——

哈［旁白］：亲上加亲，越亲越不相亲！

王：你怎么还是让愁云惨雾罩着你？

哈：陛下，太阳大，受不了这个热劲"儿"。

• 朱生豪的译文如下：

王：可是来，我的侄儿哈姆莱特，我的孩子——

哈［旁白］：超乎寻常的亲族，漠不相干的路人。

王：为什么愁云依旧笼罩在你的身上？

哈：不，陛下；我已经在太阳里晒得太久了。

这里，主要困难在于莎士比亚让哈姆莱特使用了 kin 和 kind 以及 son 和 sun 两组双关语。kind 一词又有双关意义，翻译无法完全表达，只能各译一个侧面。结果，梁和卞两先生还得用注释补足其义，朱译则连注释也没有。这种地方，能读原文注释本的人才能充分领略莎氏原意。

哈姆莱特在旁白里说：比亲戚多一点——本来我是你的侄子，现在又成了你的儿子，确实不是一般的亲戚关系啊；然而却比 kind 少一点——kind 有两层意思，一是"同类相求"的亲近感，一是"与人为善"的善意感，我同你没有共同语言，我也不知道你是安的什么心。这话只能对自己说，在舞台上假定对方是听不到的。哈姆莱特的第二句话是公开的俏皮话：哪里有什么阴云呀，我在太阳里晒得不行呢。sun 是跟 clouds 相对；太阳又意味着国王的恩宠，"你对我太好了，我怎么会阴郁呢?"sun 又跟 son 谐音，"做你的儿子，我领教得够了。"原文并不是像梁实秋所说的那样晦涩难解。可是含义太复杂，有隐藏的深层感情，所以无法译得完全。

（二）语法。有些现象，按现代英语语法的标准看，似乎是错误的，但在当时并不错，是属于中世纪英语的残余因素。例如有些动词过去分词的词尾变化、代词的所有格形式、主谓语数的不一致、关系代词和介词的用法等方面，都有一些和现在不同的情况。注释里说明了，可以举一反三去理解。

（三）词序的颠倒和穿插。词尾屈折变化较多的中世纪英语本来对词序没有严格的要求。伊丽莎白时代继承了这种习惯。同时,诗的节律和押韵要求对词序作一定的灵活处理。莎士比亚的舞台语言以鲜明、有力、生动为首要考虑,有时他就把语法和句法放在从属的地位。在激动的台词中,由于思路、感情的变化,语言也常有脱出常规的变化。这些地方,有了注释的指点,理解就容易得多。

(四)典故。莎士比亚用典很多。古希腊、罗马神话,《圣经》故事,英国民间传说,历史逸事……他都随手拈来。其中有一大部分对于英美读者来说乃是常识,但中国读者就很需要注释的帮助。

(五)文化背景。注释可以提供关于基督教义、中世纪传统观点、文艺复兴时期新的主张、英国习俗等方面的知识。

除上述以外,还有莎剧中影射时事,以及版本考据诸问题,在注释本中可以详细论述,也可以简单提及。

世界文豪莫不是语言大师,而要真正理解和欣赏一位大师的文笔,当然非读他的原著不成。出版莎士比亚注释本,首先是为了让中国读者便于买到和读到他的原著。不过我们自知现出的几十种在版本、注释和其他方面还存在不足之处,希望读者多提意见,以便今后不断改进。

裘克安

前　　言

　　《仲夏夜之梦》是莎士比亚戏剧中最受少年儿童喜爱的,也是世界上一切具有童心的人必然喜爱的。这个剧本大约于1594年初次上演,四个世纪以来一直是有特殊吸引力的剧目。有的评论家认为它当初是莎士比亚为庆祝某贵族青年结婚供私家演出而作。虽然这点并不肯定,但剧中确定了爱情和婚姻,充满了笑料,穿插以音乐、舞蹈和戏中戏,笼罩以夏夜神秘的月光和阴影,使人读了或看了便进入诗境、梦境、仙境。

　　威廉·莎士比亚(William Shakespeare 1564—1616)生活于英国商业资本主义兴盛的时期。当时统治英国的是伊丽莎白一世(1558—1603)和詹姆斯一世(1603—1625)。随着航海和通商的进展,经济的繁荣,文化艺术也迅速发达,形成英国的文艺复兴,其时间略晚于意大利的文艺复兴。莎士比亚约在22岁时以一个小镇的知识青年来到首都伦敦,传说开始曾在剧院门口为有钱的看客照料马匹,后来逐步成为戏班子的杂役、演员、剧作家和股东。他写了两首长篇叙事诗和154首十四行诗,献给贵族,公开出版或在文人雅士间传阅,因此在文坛上赢得了名气。当年写剧本还不是登大雅之堂的事业,但莎士比亚在23年间为剧团编写了37部杰出的剧本,显示了极其高超和旺盛的文学创作才能。由于剧团受大臣和国王庇护,使他能接触到上流社会;同时他与中下层人民保持密切联系,对他们的思想感情也有深入的了解。他的剧本生活内容十分丰富,情节曲折生动,人物千姿百态,思想深邃细密,激情感人肺腑。而且每个剧本几乎是一个独特的世界、意境、情调和风格各有不同,从不重复。可惜当时除本·琼生(Ben Jonson)对他有很高评价外,其余评论家一般把他看作和旁的剧作家差不多。莎士比亚悄然终老于故乡,本人的生平只留下较少的历史记载。而他的作品的意义和影响却在他死后日益彰明昭著，成为后世无数观众、读者和评论家取之不尽的宝库。

莎士比亚的许多剧本以旧的文学、历史作品为素材来源，但《仲夏夜之梦》却是他最为独创的作品之一。故事的梗概如下：雅典公爵忒修斯（古希腊传奇人物）战胜并俘虏阿玛宗女战士国女王希波吕忒之后，对她产生爱情，已订了婚期。雅典望族伊吉斯的女儿赫米娅违抗父命，不愿嫁给狄米特律斯，另爱上青年拉山德。公爵告她，她必须重新考虑，遵从父命，否则按雅典法律，可以处死，除非她在月亮女神神坛前发誓终身不嫁。赫米娅和拉山德决定私奔，相约在城外森林会合。赫米娅将此事告诉了从小的好友海丽娜。海丽娜单恋着狄米特律斯，为了讨好于他，竟把这秘密告诉了他。这样，在仲夏夜（6月23日）的新月之夜，这两女两男四个青年分别都来到了黑影憧憧的森林。这一夜这个森林正处在仙王奥布朗的管辖之下，他同仙后提泰妮娅为争夺一个小男孩拌了嘴，想捉弄她一下，命仙童迫克在她眼皮上滴一种花汁仙药，使她醒来时爱上首先看到的任何活物。同一夜，织工波顿等六个手艺工人也到森林里来排练一出为公爵婚礼助兴的小戏。在迫克的恶作剧安排下，波顿被戴上驴头假面，成为仙后迷恋的对象。仙王看到海丽娜追求狄米特律斯而受他鄙弃的可怜情状，就叫迫克把仙药也滴一些在狄米特律斯眼上。迫克却错把仙药滴在拉山德眼上，结果两个男青年都去追求海丽娜，造成一场混乱。最后仙王让迫克解除仙药的魔力，恢复了仙后和他自己的和好关系，并使狄米特律斯放弃对赫米娅的求婚，转而报答海丽娜的感情。凡人们从幻梦中醒来，公爵举行了婚礼，两对青年也随之成亲，结婚宴会之后工匠们演出了模拟短悲剧《皮拉摩斯和提斯柏》，引起观众一阵阵哄笑。这个"戏中戏"结束之后，仙王、仙后对三对伉俪的新房进行祝福，全剧告终。

《仲夏夜之梦》结构复杂而巧妙，按人物类型来分，其中包括四个层次：最空灵虚幻的是仙王、仙后、仙童迫克和四小仙；其次是公爵和他的新夫人;再次是两男两女的四个青年;最后是六个粗俗的工匠。几个层次之间发生错综的联系,发展到极端是仙后对驴头波顿的短暂迷恋。除仙后和波顿以外,四个青年也都做了梦,他们的爱情变迁既有受仙药蒙蔽的一面,也反映了年轻人性格的飘忽不定。仙王和仙后的争吵只是为了一桩琐事,本来神仙的爱情并无忠贞可言,仙后一梦之后,争吵就告解决。但是这场仙界的不和却引起天时的反常和人情的错讹。不过经这一梦,无论是梦中人还是旁观者,"大家心理上都一齐受到了影响"(希波吕忒语)。

在莎士比亚时代,剧本是属于戏班子的脚本,是手抄的,演出时经常有所改动,特别是丑角的台词;它们不是由作者一次写完作为书面文学作品出版的。现存《仲夏夜之梦》最早的印本是1600年托马斯·费希尔出版的四开本,不知道是否经莎士比亚本人看过。1619年有第二个四开本。1623年收在他的朋友海明和康德尔编的第一个对开本莎士比亚剧作全集里。《仲夏夜之梦》各版本文字出入不大。我们这里采用的是剑桥版本。

掌握了现代英语的读者,初读莎士比亚的时候会遇到许多语言方面的困难。这是由于当时英语正处在从受曲折变化复杂束缚的中世纪英语向灵活而丰富的现代英语转变的过渡时期。拉丁语和法语对英语影响很大,而莎士比亚对英语的运用又有许多革新和创造。主要的困难有如下几方面:(一)词汇异常丰富。其中许多词虽然拼法和现在一样,但具有不同的含义,不能望文生义。(二)语法上有些现象,按现代语法的标准看,似乎是错误的,但在当时并不错,是属于中世纪英语的残余因素。例如有些动词过去分词的词尾变化、代词的所有格形式、主谓语数的不一致、关系代词和介词的用法等方面都有一些和现在不同的情况。(三)词序有时颠倒错落。词尾变化较多的中世纪英语本来对词序并无严格的要求,伊丽莎白时代部分继承了这种习惯。同时诗律和押韵的要求迫使诗人对词序作一定的灵活处理,这是读诗者必然要面对的。

（四）典故多。莎士比亚常引用希腊、罗马神话和英国民间传说，在《仲夏夜之梦》里这两方面的典故杂糅在一起。有时他还联系到时事，有些可考，有些已不可考。

从文体来说，《仲夏夜之梦》丰富多彩，前面所说四类人物各用不同的文体，并有不同的语言。仙王、仙后和仙童迫克的典型诗句是一种七音节（四个重音）诗行，其中的三个音步或为抑扬格或为扬抑格，比较灵活，另外每行有一个单音步，产生一种跳跃音的效果，如：

Í do | wán der | év(e) ry | whére,

扬抑　扬　抑　扬　抑　扬

Swífter | thán the | móon es | sphére;

扬抑　　扬　抑　扬　　抑　扬

And Í | sérve the | fái ry | quéen,

抑扬扬　抑　扬抑　扬

To déw | her órbs | up ón | th(e) gréen:

抑扬　抑　扬　抑扬　　扬

这里每两行一韵，但也有押韵规律与此不同，或者不押韵的。

公爵及其新娘用的是庄严的无韵诗，即每行一般为五个抑扬格的音步，共十音节，行尾无韵，如：

Now, fáir | Hippó | ly tá, | our núp | tial hóur

Draws ón | a páce: | four háp | py dáys |

　　　bring in

四青年用的也是抑扬格五音步诗行，但有时两行一韵，有时无韵，而且比较口语化，有时相互插话，如：

Her. Why áre | you grówn | so rúde? | what chánge

　| is this,

　Sweet lóve, | —

Lys. 　　Thy lóve! | out, táw | ny Tár- | tar, óut!

工匠们说的是散文道白，俚语村言。他们演戏时的台词则是莎士比亚为讽刺旧剧陈腔滥调而写的模拟诗，有意做作或夸张，以引人发笑，体裁也多样化。

　　注释以简赅为原则。绝大多数英语注释可以拿来直接取代原文词语,构成确切的意译(paraphrase),对理解莎剧帮助较大。凡用浅近和简短的英语不易说明的问题,就用中文解说。

裘克安
于湖南师范大学外语系

A
MIDSUMMER NIGHT'S
DREAM

DRAMATIS PERSONAE

THESEUS, *Duke of Athens*
EGEUS, *father to* HERMIA
LYSANDER, ⎫ *in love with*
DEMETRIUS, ⎭ HERMIA
PHILOSTRATE, *master of the*
  revels to THESEUS
QUINCE, *a carpenter*
SNUG, *a joiner*
BOTTOM, *a weaver*
FLUTE, *a bellows-mender*
SNOUT, *a tinker*
STARVELING, *a tailor*
HIPPOLYTA, *queen of the*
  Amazons, betrothed to
  THESEUS
HERMIA, *daughter to* EGEUS,
  in love with LYS-
  ANDER
HELENA, *in love with*
  DEMETRIUS
OBERON, *king of the fairies*
TITANIA, *queen of the*
  fairies
PUCK, *or* ROBIN GOODFEL-
  LOW
PEASEBLOSSOM, ⎫
COBWEB, ⎪
MOTH, ⎬ *fairies*
MUSTARDSEED, ⎭
Other fairies attending
  their King and Queen.
  Attendants on Theseus
  and Hippolyta

注　释

Theseus [ˈθiːsjəs]：雅典公爵，也是古希腊传说中的英雄。

Egeus [iˈdʒiəs]

Lysander [laiˈsændə]

Demetrius [dəˈmiːtriəs]

Philostrate [fiˈlɔstreit]：掌宴乐之官。

Quince [kwins]：木匠（字义为"木块"）。

Snug [snʌg]：细木工人（字义为"服帖"）。

Bottom：织工（字义为"线轴"）。

Flute：手工吹风器修理工（字义为"笛子"）。

Snout [snaut]：白铁工人（字义为"猪嘴"）。

Starveling [staːvliŋ]：挨饿者（字义为"瘦鬼"）。

Hippolyta [hiˈpɔlitə]

Amazons [ˈæməzənz]：希腊神话中由女战士组成的民族。

betrothed：engaged, 订婚。

Hermia [ˈhəːmjə]

Helena [ˈhelinə]

Oberon [ˈəubərən]

Titania [tiˈtɑːniə]

Robin Goodfellow：英国民间传说中喜爱恶作剧的小仙，民谣中有关于他的描述。**Puck**：字义也为"小仙"。当代某剧说明中描述他脸和手是红褐色，穿紧身革制衣，手执连枷。

Peaseblossom：豌豆花。**pease**：是 pea 的复数。

Cobweb：蜘蛛网（中世纪英语蜘蛛叫 cop).

Mustardseed：芥菜籽。

ACT I

SCENE I

Athens. The palace of THESEUS.

Enter THESEUS, HIPPOLYTA, PHILOSTRATE, *and*
ATTENDANTS.]

THESEUS. Now, fair Hippolyta, our nuptial hour
Draws on apace; four happy days bring in
Another moon: but, O, methinks, how slow
This old moon wanes! she lingers my desires,
5 Like to a step-dame, or a dowager,
Long withering out a young man's revenue.
HIPPOLYTA. Four days will quickly steep themselves
in night;
Four nights will quickly dream away the time;
10 And then the moon, like to a silver bow
New-bent in heaven, shall behold the night
Of our solemnities.
THESEUS.   Go, Philostrate,
Stir up the Athenian youth to merriments;
Awake the pert and nimble spirit of mirth:
Turn melancholy forth to funerals;
15 The pale companion is not for our pomp.
                              [*Exit* PHILOSTRATE.
Hippolyta, I woo'd thee with my sword,
And won thy love, doing thee injuries;
But I will wed thee in another key,

I. i（第一幕第一场，后类推）（以下黑体数字为行码）

1 本剧中一部分用无韵诗，即抑扬格五音步十音节的无韵诗句，如本行的轻重音可分析如下：Now, fáir | Hip pó | ly tá | our núp | tial hóur.

3 **methinks**：it seems to me.

4 **lingers**：makes to linger, delays.

5 **Like to**：like. **dowager**：王后或贵妇人，因丈夫而获得地位并有财产继承权者，尤指其丈夫已死者。

6 **withering out**：causing to dwindle. **revenue**：收入。

11 **solemnities**：celebrations, ceremony, wedding.

13 **pert**：lively.

15 **companion**：fellow. **pomp**：splendid ceremony.

16 **thee**：旧时和诗体中第二人称单数代词 thou 的受格，这里称 thee 是表示亲爱。

16—17 Theseus 用武力征服亚马孙族，俘获了其女王 Hippolyta，然后向她求爱的。

18 **key**：声调；情调。

With pomp, with triumph and with reveling.

Enter EGEUS, HERMIA, LYSANDER, *and* DEMETRIUS.]

20 EGEUS. Happy be Theseus, our renowned duke!

THESEUS. Thanks, good Egeus: what's the news with
thee?

EGEUS. Full of vexation come I, with complaint
Against my child, my daughter Hermia.
Stand forth, Demetrius. My noble lord,

25 This man hath my consent to marry her.
Stand forth, Lysander; and, my gracious duke,
This man hath bewitch'd the bosom of my child:
Thou, thou, Lysander, thou hast given her rhymes,
And interchanged love-tokens with my child:

30 Thou hast by moonlight at her window sung,
With feigning voice, verses of feigning love;
And stolen the impression of her fantasy
With bracelets of thy hair, rings, gawds, conceits,
Knacks, trifles, nosegays, sweetmeats, messengers

35 Of strong prevailment in unharden'd youth:
With cunning hast thou filch'd my daughter's
heart;
Turn'd her obedience, which is due to me,
To stubborn harshness: and, my gracious duke,
Be it so she will not here before your Grace

40 Consent to marry with Demetrius,
I beg the ancient privilege of Athens,
As she is mine, I may dispose of her:
Which shall be either to this gentleman
Or to her death, according to our law

45 Immediately provided in that case.

THESEUS. What say you, Hermia? be advised, fair
maid;
To you your father should be as a god;
One that composed your beauties; yea, and one

19 **triumph**：public rejoicing.

21 Theseus 称 Egeus 也用 thee，因后者地位高，是公爵的好友。

27 **bosom**：heart.

28 这里 Egeus 对 Lysander 这样的小辈青年，又是生人，本应用 you，但一连用了三个 thou，是表示愤怒。

32 **stolen the impression of her fantasy**：craftily impressed yourself on her fancy.

33 **gawds**：playthings，toys. **conceits**：fancy things，trinkets.

34 **Knackes**：knick-knacks.

35 **prevailment**：power. **unharden'd**：inexperienced.

39 **Be it so**：if it be so that. **your Grace**：大人（对公爵的尊称）。

41 **beg … privilege**：take leave to exercise the right.

42 **dispose of**：处置。

43 **to**：delivering her to.

45 **Immediately**：expressly，明文。（法律用语）

46 **be advised**：take good advice，听话。

48 **composed**：fashioned，produced. **beauties**：旧时抽象名词可采取复数形式。**yea** [jei]：yes.

To whom you are but as a form in wax
50   By him imprinted and within his power
To leave the figure or disfigure it.
Demetrius is a worthy gentleman.

HERMIA. So is Lysander.

THESEUS. In himself he is;
But in this kind, wanting your father's voice,
55   The other must be held the worthier.

HERMIA. I would my father look'd but with my eyes.

THESEUS. Rather your eyes must with his judgment look.

HERMIA. I do entreat your Grace to pardon me.
I know not by what power I am made bold,
60   Nor how it may concern my modesty,
In such a presence here to plead my thoughts;
But I beseech your Grace that I may know
The worst that may befall me in this case,
If I refuse to wed Demetrius.

65   THESEUS. Either to die the death, or to abjure
For ever the society of men.
Therefore, fair Hermia, question your desires;
Know of your youth, examine well your blood,
Whether, if you yield not to your father's choice,
70   You can endure the livery of a nun;
For aye to be in shady cloister mew'd,
To live a barren sister all your life,
Chanting faint hymns to the cold fruitless moon.
Thrice-blessed they that master so their blood,
75   To undergo such maiden pilgrimage;
But earthlier happy is the rose distill'd,
Than that which, withering on the virgin thorn,
Grows, lives, and dies in single blessedness.

HERMIA. So will I grow, so live, so die, my lord,

49 but：only.

54 in this kind：in this respect. **wanting**：lacking. **voice**：vote，support，approval.

55 held：considered.

56 would：wish. **but**：only.

60 concern：befit.

61 presence：贵人面前。

65 die the death：be put to death by legal process. **abjure**：renounce on oath，发誓弃绝。

68，74 blood：passions，feelings.

69 Whether：读作 whe'r，一个音节。

70 livery：clothing，costume.

71 For aye：for ever. **shady cloister**：前面省略 the. **mew'd**：confined.

72 sister：修女。

73 fruitless moon：希腊神话中月亮女神 Diana 是贞洁的象征，无子女，故说是 fruitless.

74—75 这句可释义如下：They who so control their passions as to take such a virgins's pilgrimage are thrice-blessed.

76 这句可释义如下：The rose that is distilled（to make perfume，喻女子生儿育女）is happier in an earthly way ...

80   Ere I will yield my virgin patent up
        Unto his lordship, whose unwished yoke
        My soul consents not to give sovereignty.
        THESEUS. Take time to pause; and, by the nest
          new moon, —
        The sealing-day betwixt my love and me,
85   For everlasting bond of fellowship, —
        Upon that day either prepare to die
        For disobedience to your father's will,
        Or else to wed Demetrius, as he would;
        Or on Diana's altar to protest
90   For aye austerity and single life.
        DEMETRIUS. Relent, sweet Hermia: and, Lysander,
          yield
        Thy crazèd title to my certain right.
        LYSANDER. You have her father's love, Demetrius;
        Let me have Hermia's: do you marry him.
95 EGEUS. Scornful Lysander! true, he hath my love,
        And what is mine my love shall render him.
        And she is mine, and all my right of her
        I do estate unto Demetrius.
        LYSANDER. I am, my lord, as well derived as he,
100   As well possess'd; my love is more than his;
        My fortunes every way as fairly rank'd,
        If not with vantage, as Demetrius';
        And, which is more than all these boasts can be,
        I am beloved of beauteous Hermia:
105   Why should not I then prosecute my right?
        Demetrius, I'll avouch it to his head,
        Made love to Nedar's daughter, Helena,
        And won her soul; and she, sweet lady, dotes,
        Devoutly dotes, dotes in idolatry,
110   Upon this spotted and inconstant man.
        THESEUS. I must confess that I have heard so

80   **Ere**：before. **virgin patent**：privilege of virginity.

81—82   这两行可释义如下：to the lordship of him (anybody) to whose unwished yoke my soul does not consent to give sovereignty.

84   **sealing-day**：wedding-day, day for sealing the bond between my love and me.

89   **protest**：vow.

89—90   古希腊月神狄安娜的女信徒，在其祭坛前起誓守独身，过简朴的生活，可成为月神庙的女祭司。

92   **crazèd title**：flawed claim.

98   **estate unto**：settle on, bestow on.

99   **well derived**：well descended，出身门第好。

100   **well possess'd**：rich.

101   My fortunes are of as good a rank.

102   **with vantage**：better.

103   **which**：what.

104   **of**：by.

105   **prosecute my right**：依法要求得到我的权利。（法律用语）

106   **avouch**：affirm. **to his head**：to his face.

107   **Made love to**：曾求爱于。

108   **soul**：heart.

110   **spotted**：stained.

111   **so**：as.

much,

And with Demetrius thought to have spoke thereof;

But, being over-full of self-affairs,

My mind did lose it. But, Demetrius, come;

115 And come, Egeus; you shall go with me,

I have some private schooling for you both.

For you, fair Hermia, look you arm yourself

To fit your fancies to your father's will;

Or else the law of Athens yields you up, —

120 Which by no means we may extenuate, —

To death, or to a vow of single life.

Come, my Hippolyta: what cheer, my love?

Demetrius and Egeus, go along:

I must employ you in some business

125 Against our nuptial, and confer with you

Of something nearly that concerns yourselves.

EGEUS. With duty and desire we follow you.

[Exeunt all but LYSANDER *and* HERMIA.

LYSANDER. How now, my love! why is your cheek so pale?

How chance the roses there do fade so fast?

130 HERMIA. Belike for want of rain, which I could well

Beteem them from the tempest of my eyes.

LYSANDER. Aye me! for aught that I could ever read,

Could ever hear by tale or history,

The course of true love never did run smooth;

135 But, either it was different in blood, —

HERMIA. O cross! too high to be enthrall'd to low.

LYSANDER. Or else misgraffèd in respect of years, —

HERMIA. O spite! too old to be engaged to young.

112 And intended to speak with Demetrius about it (but failed to do so)——在这种情况下，旧时用 thought 加完成时不定式动词。spoke 是旧时 speak 的过去分词形式。

117 **For**：as for. **arm**：prepare.

122 **what cheer**：how is it with you.

123 **go along**：come along with me.

125 **Against**：in preparation for.

126 about something that closely concerns yourselves.

128 **How now**：what is the meaning of this.

130 **Belike**：perhaps.

131 **Beteem**：grant. **tempest**：指 weeping.

132 **Aye me!**：alas. **for aught**：so far as concerns anything.

135 **blood**：birth，rank.

136 **cross**：十字架，苦难。**enthrall'd**：enslaved.

137 **misgraffèd**：badly matched.

LYSANDER. Or else it stood upon the choice of friends,—

140 HERMIA. O hell! to choose love by another's eyes.

LYSANDER. Or, if there were a sympathy in choice,
War, death, or sickness did lay siege to it
Making it momentary as a sound,
Swift as a shadow, short as any dream;

145 Brief as the lightning in the collied night,
That, in a spleen, unfolds both heaven and earth,
And ere a man hath power to say 'Behold!'
The jaws of darkness do devour it up:
So quick bright things come to confusion.

150 HERMIA. If then true lovers have been ever cross'd,
It stands as an edict in destiny:
Then let us teach our trial patience,
Because it is a customary cross,
As due to love as thoughts and dreams and sighs,

155 Wishes and tears, poor fancy's followers.

LYSANDER. A good persuasion: therefore, hear me, Hermia.
I have a widow aunt, a dowager
Of great revenue, and she hath no child:
From Athens is her house remote seven leagues;

160 And she respects me as her only son.
There, gentle Hermia, may I marry thee;
And to that place the sharp Athenian law
Cannot pursue us. If thou lovest me, then,
Steal forth thy father's house to-morrow night;

165 And in the wood, a league without the town,
Where I did meet thee once with Helena,
To do observance to a morn of May,
There will I stay for thee.

HERMIA.   My good Lysander!

139 **stood upon**：depended on，rested on.

145 **collied**：darkened.

146 **spleen**：fit of anger.

150 **cross'd**：受挫折。

151 **edict**：重音在第二音节。

155 **fancy**：love.

156 **persuasion**：principle.

159 Her house is seven leagues away from Athen（1 league＝3 miles）.

160 **respects**：regards.

162 **sharp**：harsh.

164 **forth**(prep.)：from.

165 **without**：outside.

167 to celebrate May-day 英国民间有庆祝五月节的风俗，时间在一日左右，莎士比亚把它移到了希腊。

168 **stay**：wait.

I swear to thee, by Cupid's strongest bow,
170   By his best arrow with the golden head,
By the simplicity of Venus' doves,
By that which knitteth souls and prospers loves,
And by that fire which burn'd the Carthage queen,
When the false Trojan under sail was seen,
175   By all the vows that ever men have broke,
In number more than ever women spoke,
In that same place thou hast appointed me,
To-morrow truly will I meet with thee.

LYSANDER. Keep promise, love. Look, here comes Helena.

Enter HELENA.]

180   HERMIA. God speed fair Helena! whither away?

HELENA. Call you me fair? that fair again unsay.
Demetrius loves your fair: O happy fair!
Your eyes are lode-stars; and your tongue's sweet air
More tuneable than lark to shepherd's ear,
185   When wheat is green, when hawthorn buds appear.
Sickness is catching: O, were favor so,
Yours would I catch, fair Hermia, ere I go,
My ear should catch your voice, my eye your eye,
My tongue should catch your tongue's sweet melody.
190   Were the world mine, Demetrius being bated,
The rest I'd give to be to you translated.
O, teach me how you look; and with what art
You sway the motion of Demetrius' heart!

HERMIA. I frown upon him, yet he loves me still.

195   HELENA. O that your frowns would teach my smiles such skill!

169　**Cupid**：希腊神话中的小爱神，他的形象总是双眼被蒙上，玩弄的箭射中谁的心，谁就坠入情网。

171　**simplicity**：innocence. **Venus**：希望神话中的爱情女神，她出行时鸽子替她拉车。从这行开始，Hermia 改用押韵的双行诗，其他人也接用此体，直到本场之末。

172　**prospers**：makes successful. **loves**：伊丽莎白时代抽象名词可用复数。

173　**Carthage queen**：Dido，Queen of Carthage（名词作形容词用之一例）。

174　**false Trojan**：Aeneas. 他在 Troy 战争后途径 Carthage，与 Dido 相爱，后弃她乘船而去，Dido 在火葬的柴堆上自焚而死。

175　**broke**：broken.

176　**spoke**：have spoken.

182　**fair**：beauty，kind of beauty（形容词作名词用的一例）。

183　**lode-stars**：guiding stars.

184　**tuneable**：tuneful，musical.

184—185　这两行的一些名词省略了冠词，这是旧时的一种常用法。

186　**favor**：good looks. **were favor so**：would that good looks were also catching（传染，能感染到）。

188　**My**：在元音前一般用 mine，但在强调时则用 my.

190　**bated**：excepted.

191　**to be to you translated**：in order to be transformed into you.

HERMIA. I give him curses, yet he gives me love.

HELENA. O that my prayers could such affection move!

HERMIA. The more I hate, the more he follows me.

HELENA. The more I love, the more he hateth me.

200 HERMIA. His folly, Helena, is no fault of mine.

HELENA. None, but your beauty; would that fault were mine!

HERMIA. Take comfort: he no more shall see my face;

Lysander and myself will fly this place.

Before the time I did Lysander see,

205 Seem'd Athens as a paradise to me:

O, then, what graces in my love do dwell,

That he hath turn'd a heaven unto a hell!

LYSANDER. Helen, to you our minds we will unfold:

To-morrow night, when Phæbe doth behold

210 Her silver visage in the watery glass,

Decking with liquid pearl the bladed grass,

A time that lovers' flights doth still conceal,

Through Athens' gates have we devised to steal.

HERMIA. And in the wood, where often you and I

215 Upon faint primrose-beds were wont to lie,

Emptying our bosoms of their counsel sweet,

There my Lysander and myself shall meet;

And thence from Athens turn away our eyes,

To seek new friends and stranger companies.

220 Farewell, sweet playfellow; pray thou for us;

And good luck grant thee thy Demetrius!

Keep word, Lysander: we must starve our sight

From lovers' food till morrow deep midnight.

LYSANDER. I will, my Hermia.   [*Exit* HERMIA.

Helena, adieu:

225 As you on him, Demetrius dote on you!   [*Exit.*

201　None，but your beauty：It is not your fault，but the fault of your beauty.

202　he no more shall see my face：he will see my face no more，伊丽莎白时代 shall 和 will 的用法和现代有许多不同。

203　fly：flee from.

205　Seem'd Athens：这里主谓语次序颠倒，是因为前一行 Before the time 这一状语被强调而提前的缘故。

206　graces：魅力。

206—207　我的情人（Lysander）身上有多大的魅力，他竟能使天堂（雅典）变成地狱——由于在雅典无法和 Lysander 结合，雅典就变成了地狱。

209　Phæbe ['fiːbi]：希腊神话中月亮女神的另一个名字。

211　liquid pearl：dew.

212　still：always.

215　faint：淡香的。

216　counsel：secret thoughts.

219　stranger companies：company of strangers.

223　lovers'food：the sight of each other.

225　Demetrius dote on you!：前省略了 may.

HELENA. How happy some o'er other some can be!
Through Athens I am thought as fair as she.
But what of that? Demetrius thinks not so;
He will not know what all but he do know;

230 And as he errs, doting on Hermia's eyes,
So I, admiring of his qualities:
Things base and vile, holding no quantity,
Love can transpose to form and dignity:
Love looks not with the eyes, but with the mind;

235 And therefore is wing'd Cupid painted blind:
Nor hath Love's mind of any judgment taste;
Wings, and no eyes, figure unheedy haste:
And therefore is Love said to be a child,
Because in choice he is so oft beguiled.

240 As waggish boys in game themselves forswear,
So the boy Love is perjured everywhere:
For ere Demetrius look'd on Hermia's eyne,
He hail'd down oaths that he was only mine;
And when this hail some heat from Hermia felt,

245 So he dissolved, and showers of oaths did melt.
I will go tell him of fair Hermia's flight:
Then to the wood will he to-morrow night
Pursue her; and for this intelligence
If I have thanks, it is a dear expense:

250 But herein mean I to enrich my pain,
To have his sight thither and back again.   [*Exit.*

SCENE II

The same. QUINCE'S *house.*

Enter   QUINCE, SNOUT, BOTTOM, FLUTE, SNOUT,
and STARVELING.]

QUINCE. Is all our company here?

BOTTOM. You were best to call them generally, man

226　**other some**：some others.

229　**all but he**：all except him.

231　**admiring of**：这里 admiring 是 verbal noune，故接 of，它前面省略了 in.

232　**quantity**：proportion.

237　**figure**：symbolize，represent.

239　**beguiled**：受骗。

240　**waggish**：playful.

242　**eyne**：eyes(旧时多数形式，特别用在押韵的地方)。

243　**hail'd down**：poured down(下雹子)。

245　**So**：then.

249　**it is a dear expense**：possibly，"it will cost him dear"，that is，"to thank me will be painful to him".

251　**To have**：by having.

I. ii　本场是六个手艺人的谈话，除 Bottom 引用每行四音节的两段各四行的模拟式悲剧台词诗段外，全是用的散文。六人中 Bottom 较有文化，爱用一些大字，但常常用错。他们在计划排戏，参加 Theseus 婚礼的庆祝。

2　**You were best**：系从 To you it were best 变来。**generally**：应为 severally.

by man, according to the scrip.

QUINCE. Here is the scroll of every man's name,
5   which is thought fit, through all Athens, to play
in our interlude before the duke and the duchess,
on his wedding-day at night.

BOTTOM. First, good Peter Quince, say what the play
treats on; then read the names of the actors; and
10   so grow to a point.

QUINCE. Marry, our play is, The most lamentable
comedy, and most cruel death of Pyramus and
Thisby.

BOTTOM. A very good piece of work, I assure you,
and a merry. Now, good Peter Quince, call forth
15   your actors by the scroll. Masters, spread yourselves.

QUINCE. Answer as I call you. Nick Bottom, the
weaver.

BOTTOM. Ready. Name what part I am for, and
proceed.

QUINCE. You, Nick Bottom, are set down for
Pyramus.

BOTTOM. What is Pyramus? a lover, or a tyrant?

20   QUINCE. A lover, that kills himself most gallant for
love.

BOTTOM. That will ask some tears in the true
performing of it: if I do it, let the audience look
to their eyes; I will move storms, I will condole
in some measure. To the rest: yet my chief humor
25   is for a tyrant: I could play Ercles rarely, or a
part to tear a cat in, to make all split.

> The raging rocks
> And shivering shocks
> Shall break the locks
>   Of prison-gates;

3 **scrip**：piece of paper written upon.

6 **interlude**：插曲，短剧。

9 **treats on**：treats of.

11 **Marry**：旧时一种口头禅的惊叹词，系从 by the Virgin Mary 变来。

11—12 戏名是模拟当时的习惯做法，例如 1570 左右实有的一出戏叫做 A lamentable tragedy mixed full of pleasant mirth, containing the life of Cambyses, King of Persia. **lamentable**：用来形容 comedy，显然有点矛盾，这是故意如此，以达到滑稽的目的。Pyramus ['pirəməs]，Thisby ['θizbi].

15 **Masters, spread yourselves**：伙计们，坐散一些。

20 **gallant**：gallantyly，英勇地，有骑士风度地。

23 **condole**：lament.

24 **To the rest**：for the rest，此外。**humor**：inclination.

25 **Ercles**：应为 Hercules ['hə:kjuli:z]，希腊神话中的大力英雄，其实他并非暴君。**rarely**：splendidly.

30   And Phibbus' car
            Shall shine from far,
            And make and mar
             The foolish Fates.

This was lofty! Now name the rest of the players.

35   This is Ercles' vein, a tyrant's vein; a lover is more condoling.

QUINCE. Francis Flute, the bellows-mender.

FLUTE. Here, Peter Quince.

QUINCE. Flute, you must take Thisby on you.

FLUTE. What is Thisby? a wandering knight?

40   QUINCE. It is the lady that Pyramus must love.

FLUTE. Nay, faith, let not me play a woman; I have a beard coming.

QUINCE. That's all one: you shall play it in a mask, and you may speak as small as you will.

45   BOTTOM. An I may hide my face, let me play Thisby too, I'll speak in a monstrous little voice, 'Thisne, Thisne!' 'Ah, Pyramus, my lover dear! thy Thisby dear, and lady dear!'

QUINCE. No, no; you must play Pyramus: and, Flute, you Thisby.

50   BOTTOM. Well, proceed.

QUINCE. Robin Starveling, the tailor.

STARVELING. Here, Peter Quince.

QUINCE. Robin Starveling, you must play Thisby's mother. Tom Snout, the tinker.

55   SNOUT. Here, Peter Quince.

QUINCE. You, Pyramus' father: myself, Thisby's father: Snug, the joiner; you, the lion's part: and, I hope, here is a play fitted.

SNUG. Have you the lion's part written? pray you,

60   if it be, give it me, for I am slow of study.

30　Phibbus：应为 Phoebus [ˈfiːbəs]，希腊神话中的太阳神，即 Apollo. 他每天驾灿烂辉煌的马车横过天空。

33　Fates：希腊神话中司命运的三女神。

35　condoling：pathetic.

39　wandering knight?：knight-errant，游侠骑士。

41　faith：in faith, by my faith（一种惊叹词）。当时女角都由男孩子或青年担任。

44　small：细嗓子。

45　An：if.

46　Thisne：可能是 Bottom 错读 Thisby 的读音，有的评家认为此字义为 in this manner.

59　part：分角色抄出的脚本。

60　slow of study：slow in study.

QUINCE. You may do it extempore, for it is nothing
but roaring.

BOTTOM. Let me play the lion too: I will roar, that I will
do any man's heart good to hear me; I will roar, that I
will make the duke say, 'Let him roar again, let him
roar again.'

65   QUINCE. An you should do it too terribly, you would
fright the duchess and the ladies, that they would
shriek; and that were enough to hang us all.

ALL. That would hang us, every mother's son.

BOTTOM. I grant you, friends, if you should fright
70   the ladies out of their wits, they would have no
more discretion but to hang us: but I will aggravate
my voice so, that I will roar you as gently as any
sucking dove; I will roar you as 'twere any nightingale.

QUINCE. You can play no part but Pyramus; for
75   Pyramus is a sweet-faced man; a proper man, as
one shall see in a summer's day; a most lovely,
gentleman-like man: therefore you must needs play
Pyramus.

BOTTOM. Well, I will undertake it. What beard were I
best to play it in?

80   QUINCE. Why, what you will.

BOTTOM. I will discharge it in either your straw color
beard, your orange-tawny beard, your purple-in-grain
beard, or your French-crown color beard, your perfect
yellow.

QUINCE. Some of your French crowns have no hair
85   at all, and then you will play barefaced. But,
masters, here are your parts: and I am to entreat
you, request you, and desire you, to con them by
to-morrow night; and meet me in the palace wood,
a mile without the town, by moonlight; there will

62—63   **that**：so that.

66   **fright**：frighten. 第一个 **that**：so that.

70—71   **out of their wits**：神志不清。**discretion**：斟酌处理的自由。**have no more discretion but**：不得不。

71—72   **aggravate**：应为 moderate. **roar you**：roar for you.

73   **sucking**：吃奶的。**sucking dove**：雏鸽。**as 'twere**：as if it were.

75   **proper**：handsome.

78—79   **were I best**：were it best for me.

82   **orange-tawny**：dark orange. **purple-in-grain**：dyed with a fast purple.

83   **French-crown**：light yellow like a gold coin. crown 是金币名，另一意思是"头顶"，当时英国人嘲笑某些法国人因患性病而脱发，称之为"法国秃头"。

87   **con**：learn by heart.

we rehearse, for if we meet in the city, we shall
90   be dogged with company, and our devices known.
In the meantime I will draw a bill of properties,
such as our play wants. I pray you, fail me not.

BOTTOM. We will meet; and there we may rehearse most
obscenely and courageously. Take pains; be perfect:
adieu.

95   QUINCE. At the duke's oak we meet.

BOTTOM. Enough; hold or cut bow-strings.   [*Exeunt.*

91　**properties**：stage properties，道具。

94　**obscenely**：应为 obscurely. **be perfect**：know your lines well.
adieu〈法语〉：goodbye.

96　**hold or cut bow-strings**：这是箭术用语，但意思现在已查不清
楚。可能是说"遵守诺言,否则就散伙"。

ACT II

SCENE I

A wood near Athens.

Enter, from opposite sides, a FAIRY, *and* PUCK.]
PUCK. How now, spirit! whither wander you?
FAIRY. Over hill, over dale,
    Thorough bush, thorough brier,
   Over park, over pale,
5   Thorough flood, thorough fire,
I do wander everywhere,
Swifter than the moon's sphere;
And I serve the fairy queen,
To dew her orbs upon the green.
10 The cowslips tall her pensioners be:
In their gold coats spots you see;
Those be rubies, fairy favors,
In those freckles live their savors:
I must go seek some dewdrops here,
15 And hang a pearl in every cowslip's ear.
Farewell, thou lob of spirits; I'll be gone:
Our queen and all her elves come here anon.
PUCK. The king doth keep his revels here to-night:
Take heed the queen come not within his sight;
20 For Oberon is passing fell and wrath,
Because that she as her attendant hath
A lovely boy, stolen from an Indian king;
She never had so sweet a changeling:
And jealous Oberon would have the child
25 Knight of his train, to trace the forests wild;
But she perforce withholds the loved boy,
Crowns him with flowers, and makes him all her

II. i　这一场进入了仙境,全是诗体。有无韵诗,有押韵的五音步双行诗,也有押韵的三、四音步双行诗(歌谣)。

4　**pale**：fenced private land, enclosure.

7　**moon's sphere**：根据当时的天文概念,地球是不动的,月亮则嵌在一个水晶球壳上,绕地而转,24 小时一周。moon's 在这里读作 moonès。

9　**To dew**：by dewing. **her orbs**：fairy rings. 英国草地上有时出现较深色的草构成的圆圈,民间传说是仙女在此跳过舞所致,实为菌种扩散的一种现象。

10　**cowslips**：黄花草,立金花(一种长得较高的草)。初春时中央抽茎,顶上开七朵向一边略为下垂的花,花作白色管状,管端再有一朵金盏(蛋黄色花),花眼里有些深红小点。**pensioners**：gentlemen-pensioners. 类似伊丽莎白女王的 50 名年轻漂亮、衣着讲究的随从。

13　**savors**：香味。

14　**go seek**：go to seek.

15　**pearl**：dewdrop as ear-ring.

16　**lob**：country bumpkin. Puck 在仙人中是最富乡土气的。

17　**elves**：elf 的复数,小精灵。**anon**：soon.

20　**passing**：exceedingly. **fell**：angry. **wrath**：wrathful.

21　**Because that**：because.

23　**changeling**：仙人偷走或换给的儿童,这里读作三音节。

24　**would**：wishes to.

25　**train**〔集合名词〕：body of followers. **trace**：track through.

26　**perforce**：forcibly.

joy:

And now they never meet in grove or green,

By fountain clear, or spangled starlight sheen,

30   But, they do square, that all their elves for fear

Creep into acorn-cups and hide them there.

FAIRY. Either I mistake your shape and making quite,

Or else you are that shrewd and knavish sprite

Call'd Robin Goodfellow: are not you he

35   That frights the maidens of the villagery;

Skim milk, and sometimes labor in the quern,

And bootless make the breathless housewife churn;

And sometime make the drink to bear no barm;

Mislead night-wanderers, laughing at their harm?

40   Those that Hobgoblin call you, and sweet Puck,

You do their work, and they shall have good luck:

Are not you he?

PUCK.   Thou speak'st aright;

I am that merry wanderer of the night.

I jest to Oberon, and make him smile,

45   When I a fat and bean-fed horse beguile,

Neighing in likeness of a filly foal:

And sometimes lurk I in a gossip's bowl,

In very likeness of a roasted crab;

And when she drinks, against her lips I bob

50   And on her withered dewlap pour the ale.

The wisest aunt, telling the saddest tale,

Sometime for three-foot stool mistaketh me:

Then slip I from her bum, down topples she,

And 'tailor' cries, and falls into a cough:

55   And then the whole quire hold their hips and laugh;

And waxen in their mirth, and neeze, and swear

A merrier hour was never wasted there.

But, room, fairy! here comes Oberon.

FAIRY. And here my mistress. Would that he were

28 **green**：grassy land.

29 **spangled**：用发光的金属片装饰的,本指服饰,这里指星空。
sheen：brightness.

30 **square**：quarrel. **But，they do square**：without quarrelling.
that：so that.

31 **acorn-cups**：橡树子有一底托,形似小杯。

32 **Either**：读作一个音节,th 不发音。**making**：form, build.

33 **shrewd**：mischievous.

34—35 **he/ That**：the man who. **villagery**：villages, countryside；
读为三音节,e 不发音。

36 **Skim milk**：撇奶偷酪。从 Skim 起,动词不再是第三人称单
数,等于思路转为 Do not you skim? **quern**：手磨。

37 **bootless**：to no avail. **churn**：搅动制黄油用的搅乳器。

38 **sometime**：sometimes. **barm**：froth on ale, 淡色啤酒上的泡
沫。

40 **Hobgoblin**：Hob + goblin, Robin Goodfellow 的另一名字。
Hob 是从 Robert, Robin 变来。

45 **bean-fed**：fed with horse beans. **horse**：公马。**beguile**：trick.

46 **filly foal**：四岁以下的母马。

47 **gossip**：old woman.

48 **very**：true. **crab**：crab-apple, 野苹果。

49 **bob**：move up and down, rebound.

50 **dewlap**：颈部下垂的皮肉。

53 **bum**：屁股。

54 **tailor**：坐空摔跤,就叫"tailor",是旧时英国习俗,但原因不明。

55 **quire**：company.

56 **waxen**：increase. wax 加 en 是英国中部的复数形式。**neeze**：
sneeze.

57 **wasted**：spent.

58 **room**：make room, 让开。

59 **Would**：I wish.

gone!

Enter, from one side, OBERON, *with his train;*
from the other, TITANIA, *with hers.*]

60 OBERON. Ill met by moonlight, proud Titania.

TITANIA. What, jealous Oberon! Fairies, skip hence:
I have forsworn his bed and company.

OBERON. Tarry, rash wanton: am not I thy lord?

TITANIA. Then I must be thy lady: but I know

65 When thou hast stolen away from fairy land,
And in the shape of Corin sat all day,
Playing on pipes of corn, and versing love
To amorous Phillida. Why art thou here,
Come from the farthest steppe of India?

70 But that, forsooth, the bouncing Amazon,
Your buskin'd mistress and your warrior love,
To Theseus must be wedded, and you come
To give their bed joy and prosperity.

OBERON. How canst thou thus for shame, Titania,

75 Glance at my credit with Hippolyta,
Knowing I know thy love to Theseus?
Didst thou not lead him through the glimmering night
From Perigenia, whom he ravished?
And make him with fair AEgle break his faith,

80 With Ariadne and Antiopa?

TITANIA. These are the forgeries of jealousy:
And never, since the middle summer's spring,
Met we on hill, in dale, forest, or mead,
By pavèd fountain or by rushy brook,

85 Or in the beached margent of the sea,
To dance our ringlets to the whistling wind,
But with thy brawls thou hast disturb'd our sport.
Therefore the winds, piping to us in vain,
As in revenge, have suck'd up from the sea

63 **Tarry**：wait. **wanton**：person(esp. woman) of unrestrained behavior.

64—65 **know / When**：know of occasions when.

66 **Corin**：牧歌中常用的牧羊人的名字。

67 **versing love**：expressing love in verse.

68 **Phillida**：牧羊女名。

69 **Come**：past participle. **steppe**：可能是 step＝limit of travel.

70 **But**：except. **forsooth**：in truth. **bouncing**：big and healthy. **Amazon**：指 Hippolyta.

71 **buskin'd**：shod with half-boots，着半筒靴的。

72 **must**：is to.

75 **Glance at**：make sarcastic allusion to. **credit**：good reputation.

78—80 **Perigenia，AEgle，Ariadne and Antiopa**：都是希腊神话中 Theseus 的爱人。

82 **spring**：beginning.

83 **mead**：meadow.

84 **pavèd**：pebbled.

85 **in**：on. **margent**：shore.

86 **ringlets**：dances in the form of a ring. **to**：to the sound of.

90   Contagious fogs; which, falling in the land,
      Have every pelting river made so proud,
      That they have overborne their continents:
      The ox hath therefore stretch'd his yoke in vain,
      The ploughman lost his sweat; and the green corn
95   Hath rotted ere his youth attain'd a beard:
      The fold stands empty in the drowned field,
      And crows are fatted with the murrion flock;
      The nine men's morris is fill'd up with mud;
      And the quaint mazes in the wanton green,
100   For lack of tread, are undistinguishable:
      The human mortals want their winter here;
      No night is now with hymn or carol blest:
      Therefore the moon, the governess of floods,
      Pale in her anger, washes all the air,
105   That rheumatic diseases do abound:
      And thorough this distemperature we see
      The seasons alter: hoary-headed frosts
      Fall in the fresh lap of the crimson rose;
      And on old Hiems' thin and icy crown
110   An odorous chaplet of sweet summer buds
      Is, as in mockery, set: the spring, the summer,
      The childing autumn, angry winter, change
      Their wonted liveries; and the mazèd world,
      By their increase, now knows not which is which:
115   And this same progeny of evil comes
      From our debate, from our dissension;
      We are their parents and original.
   OBERON. Do you amend it, then; it lies in you:
      Why should Titania cross her Oberon?
120   I do but beg a little changeling boy,
      To be my henchman.
   TITANIA.   Set your heart at rest:
      The fairy land buys not the child of me.

90   **Contagious**：pestilential. **in**：on.

92   **overborne**：overpowered. **continents**：banks.

95   **his youth**：its young ear.

97   **murrioin**：murrain，患畜瘟的。

98   **nine men's morris**："九子戏"棋盘。牧羊人爱玩此游戏。地上画棋盘如右。两人各有九子，谁能布子在黑点上构成三点一线，就得胜。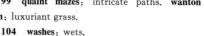

99   **quaint mazes**：intricate paths. **wanton green**：luxuriant grass.

104   **washes**：wets.

105   **rheumatic diseases**：colds，coughs，etc. which are characterized by "rheum".

106   **thorough**：through. **distemperature**：① discomposure；② bad weather.

109   **Hiems**：winter personified.

112   **childing**：fruitful. **change**：exchange.

113   **mazèd**：amazed.

114   **their increase**：the season's multiplication of crops.

116   **debate**：quarrel.

117   以上 Titania 谈到天气不正常一段，被一些评家认为是指 1594 年夏季淫雨，瘟疫流行的情况，由此推断此剧写于和演出于 1595 年，但这并非定论。**original**：origin.

118   **amend**：correct. **it lies in you**：it lies in your power.

120   **henchman**：page of honor，侍童。

121   **Set your heart at rest**：断了这个念头吧。

122   用整个仙国也买不了我这男孩。

His mother was a votaress of my order;
And, in the spiced Indian air, by night,
125   Full often hath she gossip'd by my side;
And sat with me on Neptune's yellow sands,
Marking the embarked traders on the flood;
When we have laugh'd to see the sails conceive
And grow big-bellied with the wanton wind;
130   Which she, with pretty and with swimming gait
Following, — her womb then rich with my young
      squire, —
Would imitate, and sail upon the land,
To fetch me trifles, and return again,
As from a voyage, rich with merchandise.
135   But she, being mortal, of that boy did die;
And for her sake do I rear up her boy;
And for her sake I will not part with him.
OBERON. How long within this wood intend you stay?
TITANIA. Perchance till after Theseus' wedding-day.
140   If you will patiently dance in our round,
And see our moonlight revels, go with us;
If not, shun me, and I will spare your haunts.
OBERON. Give me that boy, and I will go with thee.
TITANIA. Not for thy fairy kingdom. Fairies, away!
145   We shall chide downright, if I longer stay.

                    [*Exit* TITANIA *with her Train.*

OBERON. Well, go thy way: thou shalt not from this
      grove
Till I torment thee for this injury.
My gentle Puck, come hither. Thou rememberest
Since once I sat upon a promontory,
150   And heard a mermaid, on a dolphin's back,
Uttering such dulcet and harmonious breath,
That the rude sea grew civil at her song,
And certain stars shot madly from their spheres,

123 **votaress**：立过誓的女信徒。**order**：religious order，body of worshippers observing a common rule of life.

126 **Neptune** ['neptjuːn]：罗马神话中的海神。

127 **Marking**：watching. **traders**：trading ships.

128 **conceive**：become pregnant.

138 **stay**：to stay（to 省略）。

140 **round**：round dance.

142 **spare**：avoid.

145 **chide**：quarrel. 这行和前行押韵，达到告一段落的效果。

146 **from**：go from.

147 **injury**：insult.

149 **Since**：when.

151 **dulcet**：sweet. **breath**：voice，song.

152 **rude**：rough. **civil**：well-mannered，calm.

To hear the sea-maid's music.

PUCK.   I remember.

155 OBERON. That very time I saw, but thou couldst not,
     Flying between the cold moon and the earth,
     Cupid all arm'd: a certain aim he took
     At a fair vestal throned by the west,
     And loosed his love-shaft smartly from his bow,

160 As it should pierce a hundred thousand hearts:
     But I might see young Cupid's fiery shaft
     Quench'd in the chaste beams of the watery moon,
     And the imperial votaress passed on,
     In maiden meditation, fancy-free.

165 Yet mark'd I where the bolt of Cupid fell:
     It fell upon a little western flower,
     Before milk-white, now purple with love's wound,
     And maidens call it love-in-idleness.
     Fetch me that flower; the herb I shew'd thee once:

170 The juice of it on sleeping eye-lids laid
     Will make or man or woman madly dote
     Upon the next live creature that it sees.
     Fetch me this herb; and be thou here again
     Ere the leviathan can swim a league.

175 PUCK. I'll put a girdle round about the earth
     In forty minutes.   [*Exit.*

OBERON.   Having once this juice,
     I'll watch Titania when she is asleep,
     And drop the liquor of it in her eyes.
     The next thing then she waking looks upon,

180 Be it on lion, bear, or wolf, or bull,
     On meddling monkey, or on busy ape,
     She shall pursue it with the soul of love:
     And ere I take this charm from off her sight,
     As I can take it with another herb,

185 I'll make her render up her page to me.

157 certain：sure.

158 vestal：virgin 一般认为这是影射从未结婚的英国女王伊丽莎白一世。**by**：in.

159 love-shaft：播种爱情的箭。

160 As：as if.

161 might：could，was able to.

163 imperial：imperious，majestic. **votaress**：信奉月神，誓守独身的女子。

164 fancy-free：free from love，不受爱情的缠绕。

165 bolt：arrow.

168 love-in-idleness：pansy，heart's ease，三色堇（一种春、夏开的圆瓣小草花，紫色以外，也有黄、白色的）。

171 or … or：either … or.

172 live [laiv]：living.

174 leviathan [liˈvaiəθən]：whale.

179 thing：以后省略 that.

182 shall：will. **soul**：heart.

But who comes here? I am invisible;
And I will overhear their conference.
Enter DEMETRIUS, HELENA, *following him.*]
DEMETRIUS. I love thee not, therefore pursue me not.
Where is Lysander and fair Hermia?
190 The one I'll slay, the other slayeth me.
Thou told'st me they were stolen unto this wood,
And here am I, and wode within this wood,
Because I cannot meet my Hermia.
Hence, get thee gone, and follow me no more.
195 HELENA. You draw me, you hard-hearted adamant:
But yet you draw not iron, for my heart
Is true as steel: leave you your power to draw,
And I shall have no power to follow you.
DEMETRIUS. Do I entice you? do I speak you fair?
200 Or, rather, do I not in plainest truth
Tell you, I do not, nor I cannot love you?
HELENA. And even for that do I love you the more.
I am your spaniel; and, Demetrius,
The more you beat me, I will fawn on you:
205 Use me but as your spaniel, spurn me, strike me,
Neglect me, lose me; only give me leave,
Unworthy as I am, to follow you.
What worser place can I beg in your love, —
And yet a place of high respect with me, —
210 Than to be used as you use your dog?
DEMETRIUS. Tempt not too much the hatred of my spirit;
For I am sick when I do look on thee.
HELENA. And I am sick when I look not on you.
DEMETRIUS. You do impeach your modesty too much,
215 To leave the city, and commit yourself
Into the hands of one that loves you not;
To trust the opportunity of night

187 **conference**：conversation.

191 **were stolen**：stole 当时运动动词常用被动态。

192 **wode**：mad.

195 **adamant**：stone of excessive hardness, supposed to be magnetic.

199 **speak you fair**：speak kindly to you.

201 **nor I cannot**：因强调而不避双重否定,在当时是常见的。

214 **impeach**：discredit.

215 **To leave**：by leaving.

And the ill counsel of a desert place
With the rich worth of your virginity.

220 HELENA. Your virtue is my privilege: for that
It is not night when I do see your face,
Therefore I think I am not in the night;
Nor doth this wood lack worlds of company,
For you in my respect are all the world:

225 Then how can it be said I am alone,
When all the world is here to look on me?

DEMETRIUS. I'll run from thee and hide me in the brakes,
And leave thee to the mercy of wild beasts.

HELENA. The wildest hath not such a heart as you.

230 Run when you will, the story shall be changed:
Apollo flies, and Daphne holds the chase;
The dove pursues the griffin; the mild hind
Makes speed to catch the tiger; bootless speed,
When cowardice pursues, and valor flies.

235 DEMETRIUS. I will not stay thy questions; let me go:
Or, if thou follow me, do not believe
But I shall do thee mischief in the wood.

HELENA. Aye, in the temple, in the town, the field,
You do me mischief. Fie, Demetrius!

240 Your wrongs do set a scandal on my sex:
We cannot fight for love, as men may do;
We should be woo'd, and were not made to woo.

[*Exit* DEMETRIUS.

I'll follow thee, and make a heaven of hell,
To die upon the hand I love so well.　　　　[*Exit.*

245 OBERON. Fare thee well, nymph: ere he do leave this grove,
Thou shalt fly him, and he shall seek thy love.

Re-enter PUCK.]

Hast thou the flower there? Welcome, wanderer.

220   **privilege**：immunity. **for that**：because.

224   **in my respect**：to my mind.

227   **me**：myself.

231   **Apollo** [ə'pɔləu]：希腊神话中的太阳神。**Daphne** ['dæfni]：河神之女，被 Apollo 追求，无法逃避之际，被保护神点化为月桂树，因她曾发誓守童贞。

232   **griffin**：传说中的怪兽，鹰头、鹰翼、狮身。**hind**：母鹿。

235   **stay**：wait for.

237   **But I shall**：that I shall not.

239   **Fie**：表示斥责的惊叹词。

240   The wrongs you do me make me act in a way that disgraces my sex.

244   **To die upon**：by dying by.

245   **nymph**：女仙，女郎。

PUCK. Aye, there it is.

OBERON.   I pray thee, give it me.

    I know a bank where the wild thyme blows,

250   Where oxlips and the nodding violet grows;

    Quite over-canopied with luscious woodbine,

    With sweet musk-roses, and with eglantine:

    There sleeps Titania sometime of the night,

    Lull'd in these flowers with dances and delight;

255   And there the snake throws her enamell'd skin,

    Weed wide enough to wrap a fairy in:

    And with the juice of this I'll streak her eyes,

    And make her full of hateful fantasies.

    Take thou some of it, and seek through this grove:

260   A sweet Athenian lady is in love

    With a disdainful youth: anoint his eyes;

    But do it when the next thing he espies

    May be the lady: thou shalt know the man

    By the Athenian garments he hath on.

265   Effect it with some care that he may prove

    More fond on her than she upon her love:

    And look thou meet me ere the first cock crow.

PUCK. Fear not, my lord, your servant shall do so.

                               [Exeunt.

SCENE II

Another part of the wood.

Enter TITANIA, *with her train.*]

TITANIA. Come, now a roundel and a fairy song;

    Then, for the third part of a minute, hence;

    Some to kill cankers in the musk-rose buds;

    Some war with rere-mice for their leathern wings,

5   To make my small elves coats; and some keep back

    The clamorous owl, that nightly hoots and wonders

249   **thyme**：百里香(一种香草)。

250   **oxlips**：立金花和报春花的杂交品种。**violet**：紫罗兰。
grows：复数主语用单数动词,在当时并不少见。

251   **woodbine**：野忍冬藤。

252   **musk-roses**：野蔷薇。**eglantine**：欧石南。

253   **sometime of**：sometimes during.

255   **throws**：throws off.

256   **Weed**：garment(这是 skin 的同位语)。

257   **streak**：rub.

266   **on，upon**：of.

II. ii

1   **roundel**：大家手拉手的环形跳舞。

3   **cankers**：尺蠖等害虫。

4   **rere-mice**：bats.

At our quaint spirits. Sing me now asleep;
Then to your offices, and let me rest.

SONG.

FIRST FAIRY. You spotted snakes with double tongue,
10   Thorny hedgehogs, be not seen;
Newts and blind-worms, do no wrong,
Come not near our fairy queen.

CHORUS.

Philomel, with melody,
Sing in our sweet lullaby;
15   Lulla, lulla, lullaby, lulla, lulla, lullaby:
Never harm,
Nor spell, nor charm,
Come our lovely lady nigh;
So, good night, with lullaby.

20   FIRST FAIRY. Weaving spiders, come not here;
Hence, you long-legg'd spinners, hence!
Beetles black, approach not near;
Worm nor snail, do no offense.

CHORUS.

Philomel, with melody, etc.

25   SECOND FAIRY.   Hence, away! now all is well:
One aloof stand sentinel.

[Exeunt FAIRIES. TITANIA *sleeps.*

Enter OBERON, *and squeezes the flower on*
TITANIA'*s eyelids.]*

OBERON.   What thou seest when thou dost wake,
Do it for thy true-love take;
Love and languish for his sake:
30   Be it ounce, or cat, or bear,
Pard, or boar with bristled hair,
In thy eye that shall appear
When thou wakest, it is thy dear:
Wake when some vile thing is near.   *[Exit.*

7 **quaint**：pretty，dainty.

9 **double**：forked.

11 **Newts**：蝾螈。**blind-worms**：蛇蜥。

13 **Philomel**：希腊神话中 Thrace 王 Tereus 的小姨子，被 Tereus 奸污并割去舌头，后被众神变作夜莺。Philomel 在希腊语中意思是"爱歌者"，这里指夜莺。

18 Come near our lovely lady.

21 **long-legg'd spinners**：daddylonglegs（一种长脚双翅的昆虫）。

24 这里合唱副歌，即上面 13—19 再唱一遍。

28 **Do it**：在语法结构上是多余的，等于说 Take what thou seest … for thy true love.

30 **ounce**：lynx，山猫。

31 **Pard**：leopard.

Enter LYSANDER *and* HERMIA.]

LYSANDER. Fair love, you faint with wandering in the
35　　wood;

　　　　And to speak troth, I have forgot our way:
　　　　We'll rest us, Hermia, if you think it good,
　　　　　And tarry for the comfort of the day.
　　HERMIA. Be it so, Lysander: find you out a bed;
40　　For I upon this bank will rest my head.
　　LYSANDER. One turf shall serve as pillow for us both;
　　　　One heart, one bed, two bosoms, and one troth.
　　HERMIA. Nay, good Lysander; for my sake, my dear,
　　　　Lie further off yet, do not lie so near.
45　LYSANDER. O, take the sense, sweet, of my innocence!
　　　　Love takes the meaning in love's conference.
　　　　I mean, that my heart unto yours is knit,
　　　　So that but one heart we can make of it:
　　　　Two bosoms interchained with an oath;
50　　So then two bosoms and a single troth.
　　　　Then by your side no bed-room me deny;
　　　　For lying so, Hermia, I do not lie.
　　HERMIA. Lysander riddles very prettily:
　　　　Now much beshrew my manners and my pride,
55　　If Hermia meant to say Lysander lied.
　　　　But, gentle friend, for love and courtesy
　　　　Lie further off; in human modesty,
　　　　Such separation as may well be said
　　　　Becomes a virtuous bachelor and a maid,
60　　So far be distant: and, good night, sweet friend:
　　　　Thy love ne'er alter till thy sweet life end!
　　LYSANDER. Amen, amen, to that fair prayer, say I;
　　　　And then end life when I end loyalty!
　　　　Here is my bed: sleep give thee all his rest!
65　HERMIA. With half that wish the wisher's eyes be
　　　　press'd!

36,42 **troth**：the truth. **forgot**：lost.

45 **take the sense**：get the true meaning.

46 **conference**：conversation.

53 **riddles**：plays with words，例如上行玩弄 lie 的两个不同含义。

54 **much beshrew my manners**…：let my manners…be much cursed.

61 **Thy love ne'er alter**：May your love never change.

62 **Amen** [ɑ:'men]：so be it 是基督教祈祷中结尾和表示赞同之词。

64 **sleep give thee all his rest!**：may sleep give you all its rest. **his**：its.

[They sleep.

Enter PUCK.]

PUCK.   Through the forest have I gone,

              But Athenian found I none,

              On whose eyes I might approve

              This flower's force in stirring love.

70   Night and silence. — Who is here?

              Weeds of Athens he doth wear:

              This is he, my master said,

              Despised the Athenian maid;

              And here the maiden, sleeping sound,

75   On the dank and dirty ground.

              Pretty soul! she durst not lie

              Near this lack-love, this kill-courtesy.

              Churl, upon thy eyes I throw

              All the power this charm doth owe.

80   When thou wakest, let love forbid

              Sleep his seat on thy eyelid:

              So awake when I am gone;

              For I must now to Oberon.   *[Exit.*

Enter DEMETRIUS *and* HELENA, *running.*]

HELENA. Stay, though thou kill me, sweet Demetrius.

DEMETRIUS. I charge thee, hence, and do not haunt

85   me thus.

HELENA. O, wilt thou darkling leave me? do not so.

DEMETRIUS. Stay, on thy peril: I alone will go.   *[Exit.*

HELENA. O, I am out of breath in this fond chase!

    The more my prayer, the lesser is my grace.

90   Happy is Hermia, wheresoe'er she lies;

    For she hath blessed and attractive eyes.

    How came her eyes so bright? Not with salt tears:

    If so, my eyes are oftener wash'd than hers.

    No, no, I am as ugly as a bear;

68   **approve**：test.

69   **force**：power.

71   **Weeds**：clothes.

72   **he，my master said**：he who my master said.

79   **owe**：own.

80—81   **let love forbid/ Sleep his**(its) **seat on thy eyelid**：让爱情使你不能入睡。

86   **darkling**：in darkness 莎士比亚用此字来表示天色已晚。当时演戏是在白天，舞台并无灯光效果。

87   **on thy peril**：at your peril，take the risk if you do not.

88   **fond**：foolish.

89   **my grace**：favor granted in answer to my prayer.

95   For beasts that meet me run away for fear;
Therefore no marvel though Demetrius
Do, as a monster, fly my presence thus.
What wicked and dissembling glass of mine
Made me compare with Hermia's sphery eyne?

100   But who is here? Lysander! on the ground!
Dead? or asleep? I see no blood, no wound.
Lysander, if you live, good sir, awake.

LYSANDER. [*Awaking*] And run through fire I will for
      thy sweet sake.

     Transparent Helena! Nature shews art,

105   That through thy bosom makes me see thy heart.
Where is Demetrius? Oh, how fit a word
Is that vile name to perish on my sword!

HELENA. Do not say so, Lysander; say not so.
     What though he love your Hermia? Lord, what
     though?

110   Yet Hermia still loves you; then be content.

LYSANDER. Content with Hermia! No; I do repent
     The tedious minutes I with her have spent.
    · Not Hermia but Helena I love;
     Who will not change a raven for a dove?

115   The will of man is by his reason sway'd
And reason says you are the worthier maid.
Things growing are not ripe until their season;
So, I being young, till now ripe not to reason;
And touching now the point of human skill,

120   Reason becomes the marshal to my will,
And leads me to your eyes; where I o'erlook
Love's stories, written in love's richest book.

HELENA. Wherefore was I to this keen mockery born?
     When at your hands did I deserve this scorn?

125   Is't not enough, is't not enough, young man,
That I did never, no, nor never can,

98 **dissembling glass**: distorting mirror.

99 **sphery eyne**: star-like eyes.

104 **Transparent**: able to be seen through. **art**: magic power.

114 **reven**: 似也指 Hermia 发、肤较黑。

115 **will**: desire.

118 **ripe**: ripen.

119 And reaching now the highest point of human reason.

121 **o'erlook**: look over, read.

Deserve a sweet look from Demetrius' eye,
But you must flout my insufficiency?
Good troth, you do me wrong, good sooth, you
do,
130   In such disdainful manner me to woo.
But fare you well; perforce I must confess
I thought you lord of more true gentleness.
O, that a lady, of one man refused,
Should of another therefore be abused!   [*Exit.*
      LYSANDER. She sees not Hermia. Hermia, sleep thou
135   there;
And never mayst thou come Lysander near!
For as a surfeit of the sweetest things
The deepest loathing to the stomach brings,
Or as the heresies that men do leave
140   Are hated most of those they did deceive,
So thou, my surfeit and my heresy,
Of all be hated, but the most of me!
And, all my powers, address your love and might
To honor Helen and to be her knight!   [*Exit.*
      HERMIA. [*Awaking*] Help me, Lysander, help me! do
145   thy best
To pluck this crawling serpent from my breast!
Aye me, for pity! what a dream was here!
Lysander, look how I do quake with fear;
Methought a serpent eat my heart away,
150   And you sat smiling at his cruel prey.
Lysander! what, removed? Lysander! lord!
What, out of hearing? gone? no sound, no word?
Alack, where are you? speak, an if you hear;
Speak, of all loves! I swoon almost with fear.
155   No? then I well perceive you are not nigh;
Either death or you I'll find immediately.   [*Exit.*

129 **Good troth**, ... **sooth**: in good faith, in truth, 说真的。

131 **perforce**: of necessity.

132 **gentleness**: nobility, breeding.

133,134,140,142 of: by.

143 **address**: direct, apply.

149 **Methought**: it seemed to me that.

150 **prey**: preying.

153 **Alack**: 表示惋惜或责备的惊叹词。**an if**: if.

154 **of all loves!**: for the sake of all love. **swoon almost**: nearly swoon.

156 **Either**: 读作一个音节，th 不发音。

ACT III

SCENE I

The wood. TITANIA *lying asleep.*

Enter QUINCE, SNUG, BOTTOM, FLUTE, SNOUT, *and*
    STARVELING.]

BOTTOM. Are we all met?

QUINCE. Pat, pat; and here's a marvelous convenient
place for our rehearsal. This green plot shall be our
stage, this hawthorn-brake our tiring-house; and we
5   will do it in action as we will do it before the
duke.

  BOTTOM. Peter Quince, —

QUINCE. What sayest thou, Bully Bottom?

BOTTOM. There are things in this comedy of Pyramus
and Thisby that will never please. First, Pyramus
10 must draw a sword to kill himself; which the ladies
cannot abide. How answer you that?

SNOUT. By'r lakin, a parlous fear.

STARVELING. I believe we must leave the killing out,
when all is done.

BOTTOM. Not a whit: I have a device to make all
15 well. Write me a prologue; and let the prologue
seem to say, we will do no harm with our swords,
and that Pyramus is not killed indeed; and, for the
more better assurance, tell them that I Pyramus, am
not Pyramus, but Bottom the weaver: this will put
20 them out of fear.

QUINCE. Well, we will have such a prologue; and it
shall be written in eight and six.

BOTTOM. No, make it two more; let it be written in
eight and eight.

III. i

   2 **Pat**：on the dot. **marvelous**：marvelously.

   4 **tiring-house**：化妆室。**tire**：梳头打扮。

  11 **By'r lakin**：by our Lady. **lakin**：lady-kin, little lady，凭圣母
（马利亚）起誓。**parlous**：perilous, dangerous.

  13 **when all is done**：when all is said and done, after all.

  17—18 **the more better**：重复比较级形容词,在当时常见。

  22 **in eight and six**：in lines of eight and six syllables，民谣常用的
诗体。

25 SNOUT. Will not the ladies be afeard of the lion?

STARVELING. I fear it, I promise you.

BOTTOM. Masters, you ought to consider with yourselves:
to bring in, — God shield us! —a lion among ladies, is
a most dreadful thing; for there is not a

30 more fearful wild-fowl than your lion living: and
we ought to look to 't.

SNOUT. Therefore another prologue must tell he is
not a lion.

BOTTOM. Nay, you must name his name, and half his
face must be seen through the lion's neck; and he
himself must speak through, saying thus, or to the

35 same defect, —'Ladies,' —or, ' Fair-ladies—I
would wish You,'— or, 'I would request you,'—
or, 'I would entreat you, — not to fear, not to
tremble; my life for yours. If you think I come
hither as a lion, it were pity of my life: no, I am no

40 such thing; I am a man as other men are'; and there
indeed let him name his name, and tell them plainly,
he is Snug the joiner.

QUINCE. Well, it shall be so. But there is two hard
things; that is, to bring the moonlight into a chamber;
for, you know, Pyramus and Thisby meet by
moonlight.

45 SNOUT. Doth the moon shine that night we play our
play?

BOTTOM. A calendar, a calendar! look in the almanac;
find out moonshine, find out moonshine.

QUINCE. Yes, it doth shine that night.

BOTTOM. Why, then may you leave a casement of the
great chamber window, where we play, open, and

50 the moon may shine in at the casement.

QUINCE. Aye; or else one must come in with a bush
of thorns and a lanthern, and say he comes to dis-

28 据稗史,詹姆斯一世在继承英国王位前,还是苏格兰国王时,曾在一次假面舞剧中带进活的狮子。这里莎士比亚是暗指史实。

30 **wild-fowl**:野禽。Bottom 不懂 fowl 的意思,胡乱套用。**your**:这是俚语中的用法。

35 **defect**:Bottom 应说 effect.

38 **my life for yours**:以我的生命担保你们的生命。

39 **it were pity of**:it would be a bad thing for.

49 **great chamber**:state room,大厅。

51—52 **bush of thorns**:英国民间传说,月中人背负一捆刺柴。

52—53 **disfigure**:figure,扮演。

figure, or to present, the person of moonshine.
Then, there is another thing : we must have a wall
55   in the great chamber; for Pyramus and Thisby,
says the story, did talk through the chink of a wall.

SNOUT. You can never bring in a wall. What say you,
Bottom?

BOTTOM. Some man or other must present Wall: and
let him have some plaster , or some loam , or some
60   rough - cast about him , to signify wall ; and let him
hold his fingers thus, and through that cranny shall
Pyramus and Thisby whisper.

QUINCE. If that may be, then all is well. Come, sit
down, every mother's son, and rehearse your parts.
Pyramus , you begin : when you have spoken your
65   speech, enter into that brake: and so every one according to his cue.

Enter PUCK *behind.*]

PUCK. What hempen home-spuns have we swaggering
here, So near the cradle of the fairy queen?
What, a play toward! I'll be an auditor;
An actor too perhaps, if I see cause.

70 QUINCE. Speak, Pyramus. Thisby, stand forth.

BOTTOM. Thisby, the flowers of odious savors sweet —

QUINCE. Odorous, odorous.

BOTTOM. — odorous savors sweet:

So hath thy breath, my dearest Thisby dear.
75   But hark, a voice! stay thou but here awhile,
And by and by I will to thee appear.   [*Exit.*

PUCK. A stranger Pyramus than e'er play'd here.   [*Exit.*

FLUTE. Must I speak now?

QUINCE. Aye, marry, must you; for you must understand
he goes but to see a noise that he heard, and is to come
again.

80 FLUTE. Most radiant Pyramus, most lily-white of hue,

59   **plaster**：灰泥。**loam**：黏土和砂的混合物。

60   **rough-cast**：粗砂浆。

66   **hempen home-spuns**：土麻布（spun 是 spin 的过去分词, 喻乡下佬）。

67   **cradle**：place of repose.

68   **toward**：in preparation. **auditor**：listener，watcher.

71   **of**：a colloquialism for "have". **savors**：smells.

78   **marry**：见 I. ii 11行。

Of color like the red rose on triumphant brier,

Most brisky juvenal, and eke most lovely Jew,

    As true as truest horse, that yet would never tire,

    I'll meet thee, Pyramus, at Ninny's tomb.

85 QUINCE. 'Ninus' tomb,' man: why, you must not speak
that yet; that you answer to Pyramus: you speak all
your part at once, cues and all. Pyramus enter: your
cue is past; it is, 'never tire.'

FLUTE. O, — As true as truest horse, that yet would
never tire.

Re-enter PUCK, *and* BOTTOM *with an ass's head.*]

90 BOTTOM. If I were, fair Thisby, I were only thine.

QUINCE. O monstrous! O strange! we are haunted.

    Pray, masters! fly, masters! Help!

                  [*Exeunt* QUINCE, SNUG, FLUTE, SNOUT,
                            and STARVELING.

PUCK. I'll follow you, I'll lead you about a round,

    Through bog, through bush, through brake, through
      brier:

95   Sometime a horse I'll be, sometime a hound,

      A hog, a headless bear, sometime a fire;

    And neigh, and bark, and grunt, and roar, and
      burn,

    Like horse, hound, hog, bear, fire, at every turn.
                            [*Exit.*

BOTTOM. Why do they run away? this is a knavery of

100   them to make me afeard.

Re-enter SNOUT.]

SNOUT. O Bottom, thou art changed! what do I see on
thee?

BOTTOM. What do you see? You see an ass - head of your
own, do you?   [*Exit* SNOUT.

Re-enter QUINCE.]

QUINCE. Bless thee, Bottom! bless thee! thou art trans-

82 **brisky juvenal**：brisk youth. **eke**：also. Jew 约是 jewel 的简缩形式，为了凑韵。

84 **Ninny**：fool.

85 **Ninus**：神话中 Nineveh 城的创建者。

87 **cues**：提示的台词。

93 **round**：roundabout way.

95，96 **sometime**：sometimes.

104 **translated**：transformed.

lated.   [*Exit.*

105   BOTTOM. I see their knavery: this is to make an ass
of me; to fright me, if they could. But I will not stir
from this place, do what they can: I will walk up and
down here, and I will sing, that they shall hear I am
not afraid.   [*Sings.*

The ousel cock so black of hue,

110   With orange-tawny bill,

The throstle with his note so true,

The wren with little quill.

TITANIA. [*Awaking*] What angel wakes me from my
flowery bed?

BOTTOM. [*Sings*]

115   The finch, the sparrow, and the lark,

The plain-song cuckoo gray,

Whose note full many a man doth mark,

And dares not answer nay; —

for, indeed, who would set his wit to so foolish a bird?

120   who would give a bird the lie, though he cry 'cuckoo'
never so?

TITANIA. I pray thee, gentle mortal, sing again:

Mine ear is much enamour'd of thy note;

So is mine eye enthralled to thy shape;

And thy fair virtue's force perforce doth move me

125   On the first view to say, to swear, I love thee.

BOTTOM. Methinks, mistress, you should have little
reason for that: and yet, to say the truth, reason
and love keep little company together now-a-days;
the more the pity , that some honest neighbors will

130   not make them friends. Nay, I can gleek upon
occasion.

TITANIA. Thou art as wise as thou art beautiful.

BOTTOM. Not so, neither: but if I had wit enough to get
out of this wood, I have enough to serve mine own

108   **that they shall**：so that they will.

109   **ousel**：blackbird，乌鸦。它和下面所提到的都是英国常见的
鸟。

   111   **throstle**：thrush，画眉。

   112   **wren**：鹪鹩。

   115   **finch**：雀科中的鸣禽。**lark**：云雀。

   116   **cuckoo**：杜鹃鸟。杜鹃的一个习性是把蛋放在其他鸟的巢
里，因此旧时风俗，当奸夫走近时，旁人就喊"Cuckoo"（杜鹃来了），以警
告该家的丈夫。后来由此演化，又把妻子与人通奸的丈夫叫做 cuckold
（类似中国的乌龟、王八）。

   119   **set his wit to**：use his intelligence to answer.

   120   **give a bird the lie**：同 118 行的 answer nay，对杜鹃回答："你
撒谎"。

   122   **enamour'd of**：inspired with love of.

   124   **thy fair virtue's force**：the power of your excellent qualities.

   130   **gleek**：make a satirical joke. **upon occasion**：occasionally.

turn.

TITANIA. Out of this wood do not desire to go:

135 Thou shalt remain here, whether thou wilt or no.

I am a spirit of no common rate:

The summer still doth tend upon my state;

And I do love thee: therefore, go with me;

I'll give thee fairies to attend on thee;

140 And they shall fetch thee jewels from the deep,

And sing while thou on pressed flowers dost sleep:

And I will purge thy mortal grossness so,

That thou shalt like an airy spirit go.

Peaseblossom! Cobweb! Moth! and Mustardseed!

Enter PEASEBLOSSOM, COBWEB, MOTH, *and* MUSTARDSEED].

FIRST FAIRY. Ready.

SECOND FAIRY. 　　And I.

THIRD FAIRY. 　　　　And I.

FOURTH FAIRY. 　　　　　And I.

145 ALL. 　　　　　　　Where shall we go?

TITANIA. Be kind and courteous to this gentleman;

Hop in his walks, and gambol in his eyes;

Feed him with apricocks and dewberries,

With purple grapes, green figs, and mulberries;

150 The honey-bags steal from the humble-bees,

And for night-tapers crop their waxen thighs,

And light them at the fiery glow-worm's eyes,

To have my love to bed and to arise;

And pluck the wings from Painted butterflies,

155 To fan the moonbeams from his sleeping eyes:

Nod to him, elves, and do him courtesies.

FIRST FAIRY. Hail, mortal!

SECOND FAIRY. Hail!

THIRD FAIRY. Hail!

160 FOURTH FAIRY. Hail!

BOTTOM. I cry your worships mercy, heartily: I beseech

133 **turn**: purpose. 此句意为,我有足够本领养活自己。

137 **still**: always, continually. **doth tend upon my state**: waits upon my high position.

140 旧时相信珠宝都出产在海底。

147 **in his eyes**: in his sight, in his presence.

148 **apricocks**: apricots, 杏。 **dewberries**: 一种黑莓。

150 **humble-bees**: 野蜂。

151 **night-tapers**: 细蜡烛。 **crop**: collect wax from.

161 **cry…mercy**: beg pardon (for asking you your names). **your workship**: title used to show respect for person of higher station, 足下。

your worship's name.

COBWEB. Cobweb.

BOTTOM. I shall desire you of more acquaintance, good
165   Master Cobweb: if I cut my finger, I shall make bold
with you. Your name, honest gentleman?

PEASEBLOSSOM. Peaseblossom.

BOTTOM. I pray you, commend me to Mistress Squash,
your mother, and to Master Peascod, your father.
Good Master Peaseblossom, I shall desire you of
170   more acquaintance too. Your name, I beseech you,
Sir?

MUSTARDSEED. Mustardseed.

BOTTOM. Good Master Mustardseed, I know your
patience well: that same cowardly, giant-like ox-beef
175   hath devoured many a gentleman of your house: I
promise you your kindred hath made my eyes water ere
now. I desire your more acquaintance, good Master
Mustardseed.

TITANIA. Come, wait upon him; lead him to my bower.
The moon methinks looks with a watery eye;
180   And when she weeps, weeps every little flower,
Lamenting some enforced chastity.
Tie up my love's tongue, bring him silently. [*Exeunt.*

SCENE II

Another part of the wood.

Enter OBERON.]

OBERON. I wonder if Titania be awaked;
Then, what it was that next came in her eye,
Which she must dote on in extremity.

Enter PUCK.]

Here comes my messenger.

How now, mad spirit!

164   **desire you of more acquaintance**：desire more acquaintance of you.

165   **make bold with you**：take liberties with you，对你放肆。旧俗，割破手时，用蛛网贴伤口以止血。

168   **Squash**：未熟的豆荚。

169   **Peascod**：已熟的豆荚。

174   **ox-beef**：beef-ox，菜牛。

176   **promise**：assure. **made my eyes water**：芥末的辣味使我流泪。

180   小花流泪指露水，迷信认为露来自月亮。

181   **enforced chastity**：chastity being violated. 月神 Diana 是贞洁的守护神。

182   这一行指制止 Bottom 出声，可见他曾不时作驴叫。

III. ii

3   **in extremity**：in the highest degree.

5   What night-rule now about this haunted grove?

PUCK. My mistress with a monster is in love.

Near to her close and consecrated bower,

While she was in her dull and sleeping hour,

A crew of patches, rude mechanicals,

10   That work for bread upon Athenian stalls,

Were met together to rehearse a play,

Intended for great Theseus' nuptial-day.

The shallowest thick-skin of that barren sort,

Who Pyramus presented, in their sport

15   Forsook his scene, and enter'd in a brake:

When I did him at this advantage take,

An ass's nowl I fixed on his head:

Anon his Thisbe must be answered,

And forth my mimic comes. When they him spy,

20   As wild geese that the creeping fowler eye,

Or russet-pated choughs, many in sort,

Rising and cawing at the gun's report,

Sever themselves and madly sweep the sky,

So, at his sight, away his fellows fly;

25   And, at our stamp, here o'er and o'er one falls;

He murder cries, and help from Athens calls.

Their sense thus weak, lost with their fears thus
      strong,

Made senseless things begin to do them wrong;

For briers and thorns at their apparel snatch;

30   Some sleeves, some hats, from yielders all things
        catch.

I led them on in this distracted fear,

And left sweet Pyramus translated there:

When in that moment, so it came to pass,

Titania waked, and straightway loved an ass.

35   OBERON. This falls out better than I could devise.

But hast thou yet latch'd the Athenian's eyes

5   **night-rule**: diversion of the night.

7   **close**: private, secret.

9   **patches**: fools, clowns. **rude mechanicals**: rough working men.

10   **upon**: at.

13   **thick-skin**: blockhead. **barren sort**: stupid group.

15   **Forsook his scene**: left his stage.

17   **nowl**: head.

18   **Anon**: soon.

19   **mimic**: burlesque actor. **spy**: see.

20   **fowler**: 猎禽者。**eye**: sec.

21   **russet-pated choughts**: 褐头的红嘴山鸦。**sort**: flock.

22   **cawing**: 鸦叫。**report**: sound of explosion.

23   **Sever themselves**: go separate ways.

25   **our stamp**: my stamping.

27   **lost**: bewildered.

30   **from yielders all things catch**: everything preys on yielders (timid people).

32   **translated**: transformed.

33   **in**: at.

34，40   **waked**: woke 的旧形式。

36   **latch'd**: caught and held fast as by a charm.

With a love-juice, as I did bid thee do?

PUCK. I took him sleeping, — that is finish'd too, —
And the Athenian woman by his side;

40   That, when he waked, of force she must be eyed.

Enter HERMIA *and* DEMETRIUS.]

OBERON. Stand close: this is the same Athenian.

PUCK. This is the woman, but not this the man.

DEMETRIUS. O, why rebuke you him that loves you so?
Lay breath so bitter on your bitter foe.

45 HERMIA. Now I but chide; but I should use thee worse,
For thou, I fear, hast given me cause to curse.
If thou hast slain Lysander in his sleep,
Being o'er shoes in blood, plunge in the deep,
And kill me too.

50   The sun was not so true unto the day
As he to me: would he have stolen away
From sleeping Hermia? I'll believe as soon
This whole earth may be bored, and that the moon
May through the centre creep, and so displease

55 Her brother's noontide with the Antipodes.
It cannot be but thou hast murder'd him;
So should a murderer look; so dead, so grim.

DEMETRIUS. So should the murder'd look; and so should I,
Pierced through the heart with your stern cruelty:

60 Yet you, the murderer, look as bright, as clear,
As yonder Venus in her glimmering sphere.

HERMIA. What's this to my Lysander? where is he?
Ah, good Demetrius, wilt thou give him me?

DEMETRIUS. I had rather give his carcass to my hounds.

65 HERMIA. Out , dog ! out , cur ! thou drivest me past the bounds
Of maiden's patience. Hast thou slain him, then?
Henceforth be never number'd among men!

40   **That**: so that. **of force**: of necessity.

41   **close**: free from observation, concealed.

45   **should**: ought to.

45—47   Hermia 对 Demetrius 称 thou，是生气的表现。

48   **o'er shoes**: deep enought to cover the shoes.

53   **bored**: 穿孔。

55   **Her brother**: the sun. **Antipodes**: those who dwell on the opposite side of the earth.

57   **dead**: deadly.

61   **Venus**: 金星，同时是希腊神话中的爱情女神。 **sphere**: orbit.

O, once tell true, tell true, even for my sake!
Durst thou have look'd upon him being awake,
70 And hast thou kill'd him sleeping? O brave touch!
Could not a worm, an adder, do so much?
An adder did it; for with doubler tongue
Than thine, thou serpent, never adder stung.

DEMETRIUS. You spend your passion on a misprised
mood:
75 I am not guilty of Lysander's blood;
Nor is he dead, for aught that I can tell.

HERMIA. I pray thee, tell me then that he is well.

DEMETRIUS. An if I could, what should I get therefore?

HERMIA. A privilege, never to see me more.
80 And from thy hated presence part I so:
See me no more, whether he be dead or no.   [*Exit*.

DEMETRIUS. There is no following her in this fierce vein:
Here therefore for a while I will remain.
So sorrow's heaviness doth heavier grow
85 For debt that bankrupt sleep doth sorrow owe;
Which now in some slight measure it will pay,
If for his tender here I make some stay.
                   [*Lies down and sleeps*.

OBERON. What hast thou done? thou hast mistaken quite,
And laid the love-juice on some true-love's sight:
90 Of thy misprision must perforce ensue
Some true love turn'd, and not a false turn'd true.

PUCK. Then fate o'er-rules, that, one man holding
troth,
A million fail, confounding oath on oath.

OBERON. About the wood go swifter than the wind,
95 And Helena of Athens look thou find:
All fancy-sick she is and pale of cheer,
With sighs of love, that costs the fresh blood dear:
By some illusion see thou bring her here:

70 brave touch：fine stroke（讽刺的反话）。

71 worm, adder：snake.

72 doubler：more forked, more double-dealing.

74 spend：waste. **misprised mood**：anger based on misunderstanding.

78 An if：if. **therefore**：for that.

81 whether：读作一个音节 whe'r.

84 heavier：此处有"心情沉重"和"瞌睡"双重意义。

85 For…：because of the debt that bankrupt sleep owes to sorrow (sleeplessness caused by sorrow).

86 Which：指 debt. **it**：指 sleep.

87 If I stay a while here to give sorrow's offer of payment(to sleep).

90 Of：from. **misprision**：mistake.

91 turn'd：changed (to).

92—93 If so, fate has taken a hand, since for one man who is true in love there are a million who fail, breaking oath after oath.

95 look：take care.

96 fancy-sick：love-sick. **cheer**：face.

97 旧时认为，每叹一口气，要损失一滴血。主语 sighs 为复数，但谓语用单数。

I'll charm his eyes against she do appear.

100 PUCK. I go, I go; look how I go,

Swifter than arrow from the Tartar's bow.   [*Exit.*

OBERON.   Flower of this purple dye,

Hit with Cupid's archery,

Sink in apple of his eye.

105   When his love he doth espy,

Let her shine as gloriously

As the Venus of the sky.

When thou wakest, if she be by,

Beg of her for remedy.

Re-enter PUCK.]

110 PUCK.   Captain of our fairy band,

Helena is here at hand;

And the youth, mistook by me,

Pleading for a lover's fee.

Shall we their fond pageant see?

115   Lord, what fools these mortals be!

OBERON.   Stand aside: the noise they make

Will cause Demetrius to awake.

PUCK.   Then will two at once woo one;

That must needs be sport alone;

120   And those things do best please me

That befall preposterously.

Enter LYSANDER *and* HELENA.]

LYSANDER. Why should you think that I should woo in
          scorn?

Scorn and derision never come in tears:

Look, when I vow, I weep; and vows so born,

125   In their nativity all truth appears.

How can these things in me seem scorn to you,

Bearing the badge of faith, to prove them true?

HELENA. You do advance your cunning more and more.

When truth kills truth, O devilish-holy fray!

99　**against**：against the time when.

101　**Tartar**：鞑靼人（泛指东方游牧民族）。

104　（the）**apple of his eye**：his eye pupil，瞳孔。

105　**espy**：spy，see.

112　**mistook**：mistaken.

113　**fee**：payment.

114　**fond pageant**：foolish play.

119　**alone**：above all things.

121　**preposterously**：against the natural order of things.

124　**Look，when**：whenever.

124—125　All truth appears in the nativity of such vows.

127　**badge of faith**：指上文的 tears.

129　**devilish-holy fray**：a confict that is at once devilish and holy.

130 These vows are Hermia's: will you give her o'er?
Weigh oath with oath, and you will nothing weigh:
Your vows to her and me, put in two scales,
Will even weigh; and both as light as tales.
LYSANDER. I had no judgment when to her I swore.
135 HELENA. Nor none, in my mind, now you give her o'er.
LYSANDER. Demetrius loves her, and he loves not you.
DEMETRIUS. [*Awaking*] O Helen, goddess, nymph,
perfect, divine!
To what, my love, shall I compare thine eyne?
Crystal is muddy. O, how ripe in show
140 Thy lips, those kissing cherries, tempting grow!
That pure congealed white, high Taurus' snow,
Fann'd with the eastern wind, turns to a crow
When thou hold'st up thy hand: O, let me kiss
This princess of pure white, this seal of bliss!
145 HELENA. O spite! O hell! I see you all are bent
To set against me for your merriment:
If you were civil and knew courtesy,
You would not do me thus much injury.
Can you not hate me, as I know you do,
150 But you must join in souls to mock me too?
If you were men, as men you are in show,
You would not use a gentle lady so;
To vow, and swear, and superpraise my parts,
When I am sure you hate me with your hearts.
155 You both are rivals, and love Hermia;
And now both rivals, to mock Helena:
A trim exploit, a manly enterprise,
To conjure tears up in a poor maid's eyes
With your derision! none of noble sort
160 Would so offend a virgin, and extort
A poor soul's patience, all to make you sport.
LYSANDER. You are unkind, Demetrius; be not so;

130　**give her o'er**：abandon her.

133　**even weigh**：weigh even 等于 131 行的 nothing weigh，两相抵销，没有重量。**tales**：瞎编的故事。

141　**Taurus**：土耳其一山脉。

144　**princess**：paragon，完美的典范。**seal**：token（均指 Helena 的手）。

145　**hell**：轻微的咒骂词。

150　**join in souls**：join in heart and mind.

152　**use**：treat. **gentle**：noble.

153　**parts**：qualities.

157　**trim**：fine（讽刺的反话）。

159　**sort**：class of people.

160—161　**extort ... patience**：make impatient. **make you sport**：make pastime for you.

For you love Hermia; this you know I know:
And here, with all good will, with all my heart,
165　In Hermia's love I yield you up my part;
And yours of Helena to me bequeath,
Whom I do love, and will do till my death.
HELENA. Never did mockers waste more idle breath.
DEMETRIUS. Lysander, keep thy Hermia; I will none:
170　If e'er I loved her, all that love is gone.
My heart to her but as guest-wise sojourn'd,
And now to Helen is it home return'd,
There to remain.
LYSANDER. Helen, it is not so.
175　DEMETRIUS. Disparage not the faith thou dost not know,
Lest, to thy peril, thou aby it dear.
Look, where thy love comes; yonder is thy dear.
Re-enter HERMIA.]
HERMIA. Dark night, that from the eye his function
takes,
The ear more quick of apprehension makes;
180　Wherein it doth impair the seeing sense,
It pays the hearing double recompense.
Thou are not by mine eye, Lysander, found;
Mine ear, I thank it, brought me to thy sound.
But why unkindly didst thou leave me so?
185　LYSANDER. Why should he stay, whom love doth press to
go?
HERMIA. What love could press Lysander from my side?
LYSANDER. Lysander's love, that would not let him bide,
Fair Helena, who more engilds the night
Than all yon fiery oes and eyes of light.
190　Why seek'st thou me? could not this make thee
know,
The hate I bare thee made me leave thee so?
HERMIA. You speak not as you think: it cannot be.

169 **I will none**: I want nothing to do with her.

171 My heart only visited her for a short time as a guest.

176 For fear that, at your risk, you pay a costly penalty for it.

178 **his**: its.

180 **Wherein**: though.

183 **I thank it**: I think.

188 **engilds**: brightens with golden light.

189 **yon**: yonder. **oes and eyes**: stars.

HELENA. Lo, she is one of this confederacy!
Now I perceive they have conjoin'd all three
195 To fashion this false sport, in spite of me.
Injurious Hermia! most ungrateful maid!
Have you conspired, have you with these contrived
To bait me with this foul derision?
Is all the counsel that we two have shared,
200 The sisters' vows, the hours that we have spent,
When we have chid the hasty-footed time
For parting us, — O, is all forgot?
All school-days' friendship, childhood innocence?
We, Hermia, like two artificial gods,
205 Have with our needles created both one flower,
Both on one sampler, sitting on one cushion,
Both warbling of one song, both in one key;
As if our hands, our sides, voices, and minds,
Had been incorporate. So we grew together,
210 Like to a double cherry, seeming parted,
But yet an union in partition;
Two lovely berries moulded on one stem;
So, with two seeming bodies, but one heart;
Two of the first, like coats in heraldry,
215 Due but to one, and crowned with one crest.
And will you rent our ancient love asunder,
To join with men in scorning your poor friend?
It is not friendly, 'tis not maidenly:
Our sex, as well as I, may chide you for it,
220 Though I alone do feel the injury.
HERMIA. I am amazed at your passionate words.
I scorn you not: it seems that you scorn me.
HELENA. Have you not set Lysander, as in scorn,
To follow me and praise my eyes and face?
225 And made your other love, Demetrius,
Who even but now did spurn me with his foot,

195   **in spite of me**：to spite me.

198   **bait**：torment.

204   **artificial**：artistically skiful.

206   **sampler**：绣花样本。

209   **incorporate**：of one body.

210   **Like to**：like.

212   **moulded**：formed, shaped.

214   **heraldry**：纹章学。**coats**：coat of arms 英国高贵家族的纹章,原来是画在盾牌上,后成为单独的饰物。**the first**：描述纹章绘制法时最初提到的颜色。

215   **crest**：纹章的顶饰;谓虽然而一颜色出现两次,但属于同一家族,其顶饰是一个。

216   **rent**：rend, tear. **ancient**：past.

226   **even but**：even.

To call me goddess, nymph, divine and rare,
Precious, celestial? Wherefore speaks he this
To her he hates? and wherefore doth Lysander
230 Deny your love, so rich within his soul,
And tender me, forsooth, affection,
But by your setting on, by your consent?
What though I be not so in grace as you,
So hung upon with love, so fortunate,
235 But miserable most, to love unloved?
This you should pity rather than despise.

HERMIA. I understand not what you mean by this.

HELENA. Aye, do, persever, counterfeit sad looks,
Make mouths upon me when I turn my back;
240 Wink each at other; hold the sweet jest up:
This sport, well carried, shall be chronicled.
If you have any pity, grace, or manners,
You would not make me such an argument.
But fare ye well: 'tis partly my own fault;
245 Which death or absence soon shall remedy.

LYSANDER. Stay, gentle Helena; hear my excuse;
My love, my life, my soul, fair Helena!

HELENA. O excellent!

HERMIA.   Sweet, do not scorn her so.

DEMETRIUS. If she cannot entreat, I can compel.

250 LYSANDER. Thou canst compel no more than she entreat:
Thy threats have no more strength than her weak
                    prayers.
Helen, I love thee; by my life, I do:
I swear by that which I will lose for thee,
To prove him false that says I love thee not.

255 DEMETRIUS. I say I love thee more than he can do.

LYSANDER. If thou say so, withdraw, and prove it too.

DEMETRIUS. Quick, come!

HERMIA.   Lysander, whereto tends all this?

231   **forsooth**：in truth（讽刺的语气，连下"所谓的爱情"）。

232   **But**：if not.

233   **grace**：favor.

234   **hung upon**：listened to with attention.

238   **persever**：persevere 的一种旧时形式，重音在第二音节，意为"坚持做下去"。

240   **each at other**：at each other. **hold the sweet jest up**：keep up the joke.

241   **carried**：conducted，managed.

243   **argument**：subject of joking.

244   **ye**：you 受格的一种形式。

253   **by that**：by my life.

256   **withdraw, and prove it too**：let us go and decide the matter by a duel. **withdraw**：拔出剑来。

257   **whereto tends all this?**：where will all this lead to?

LYSANDER.Away, you Ethiope!

DEMETRIUS.   No, no, sir; still

Seem to break loose; take on as you would follow,

260   But yet come not; you are a tame man, go!

LYSANDER. Hang off, thou cat, thou burr! vile thing, let
loose,

Or I will shake thee from me like a serpent!

HERMIA. Why are you grown so rude? what change is
this?

Sweet love, —

LYSANDER. Thy love! out, tawny Tartar, out!

265   Out, loathed medicine! hated potion, hence!

HERMIA. Do you not jest?

HELENA.   Yes, sooth; and so do you.

LYSANDER. Demetrius, I will keep my word with thee.

DEMETRIUS. I would I had your bond, for I perceive

A weak bond holds you; I'll not trust your word.

270   LYSANDER. What, should I hurt her, strike her, kill
her dead?

Although I hate her, I'll not harm her so.

HERMIA. What, can you do me greater harm than hate?

Hate me! wherefore? O me! what news, my love!

Am not I Hermia? are not you Lysander?

275   I am as fair now as I was erewhile.

Since night you loved me; yet since night you left me;

Why, then you left me, — O, the gods forbid! —

In earnest, shall I say?

LYSANDER.   Aye, by my life;

And never did desire to see thee more.

280   Therefore be out of hope, of question, of doubt;

Be certain, nothing truer; 'tis no jest

That I do hate thee, and love Helena.

HERMIA. O me! you juggler! you canker-blossom!

You thief of love! what, have you come by night

258   Ethiope：埃塞俄比亚人，指 Hermia 皮肤较黑。

258—259   这两行原来文字有错讹，考据家有各种不同的猜想读法。**still**：always.

259—260   take on as：act as if. 你(Lysander) 总是装作脱离 Hermia，装作要跟我(去决斗)，但却不来；你是个胆小鬼，走啊！ **tame**：spiritless.

261   Hang off：leave, go. **cat**：骂人为"猫"，是轻蔑之词。**burr**：bur 牛蒡(带刺的草籽，善粘人衣)。

264   tawny Tartar：黄褐色皮肤的鞑靼人。

265   medicine! potion：都指毒药。

268   bond：pledge, tie. 这里指 Hermia 拖住了 Lysander.

275   erewhile：before.

283   canker-blossom：worm that cankers (使萎落) the blossom (of love). 这里 juggler 指 Lysander 变心。

      And stolen my love's heart from him?

285 HELENA.   Fine, i'faith!

      Have you no modesty, no maiden shame,

      No touch of bashfulness? What, will you tear

      Impatient answers from my gentle tongue?

      Fie, fie! you counterfeit, you puppet, you!

290 HERMIA. Puppet? why so? aye, that way goes the game.

      Now I perceive that she hath made compare

      Between our statures; she hath urged her height;

      And with her personage, her tall personage,

      Her height, forsooth, she hath prevail'd with him.

295   And are you grown so high in his esteem,

      Because I am so dwarfish and so low?

      How low am I, thou painted maypole? speak;

      How low am I? I am not yet so low

      But that my nails can reach unto thine eyes.

300 HELENA. I pray you, though you mock me, gentlemen,

      Let her not hurt me: I was never curst;

      I have no gift at all in shrewishness;

      I am a right maid for my cowardice:

      Let her not strike me. You perhaps may think,

305   Because she is something lower than myself,

      That I can match her.

      HERMIA.   Lower! hark, again.

      HELENA. Good Hermia, do not be so bitter with me,

      I evermore did love you, Hermia,

      Did ever keep your counsels, never wrong'd you;

310   Save that, in love unto Demetrius,

      I told him of your stealth unto this wood.

      He follow'd you; for love I follow'd him;

      But he hath chid me hence and threaten'd me

      To strike me, spurn me, nay, to kill me too:

315   And now, so you will let me quiet go,

      To Athens will I bear my folly back,

291 **compare**：comparison.

292 **urged**：put forward a strong argument for.

293 **personage**：personal appearance.

297 **maypole**：按英国人习俗在乡间欢度五月节时，在空场中央竖立很高的五月柱，乡亲们围柱而舞。柱上涂彩，系以彩旗。这里把瘦长个子的 Helena 比作五月柱。

301 **curst**：malignant.

303 **right**：real.

309 **keep your counsels**：keep your secrets.

310 **Save**：except.

311 **stealth**：stealing away.

313 **chid**：driven away with scolding.

315 **so**：provided that. **quiet**：quietly.

And follow you no further: let me go:

You see how simple and how fond I am.

HERMIA. Why, get you gone: who is't that hinders
you?

320　HELENA. A foolish heart, that I leave here behind.

HERMIA. What, with Lysander?

HELENA. With Demetrius.

LYSANDER. Be not afraid; she shall not harm thee,
Helena.

DEMETRIUS. No, sir, she shall not, though you take her
part.

HELENA. O, when she's angry, she is keen and shrewd!

325　She was a vixen when she went to school;

And though she be but little, she is fierce.

HERMIA. Little again! nothing but low and little!

Why will you suffer her to flout me thus?

Let me come to her.

LYSANDER. 　　　　Get you gone, you dwarf;

330　You minimus, of hindering knot-grass made;

You bead, you acorn.

DEMETRIUS. 　　　　You are too officious

In her behalf that scorns your services.

Let her alone: speak not of Helena;

Take not her part; for, if thou dost intend

335　Never so little show of love to her,

Thou shalt aby it.

LYSANDER. 　　　Now she holds me not;

Now follow, if thou darest, to try whose right,

Of thine or mine, is most in Helena.

DEMETRIUS. Follow! nay, I'll go with thee, cheek by jole.

[*Exeunt* LYSANDER *and* DEMETRIUS.

340　HERMIA. You, mistress, all this coil is 'long of you;

Nay, go not back.

324   **keen**：bitter, sharp. **shrewd**：shrewish.

330   **minimus**：tiny creature. **knot-grass**：两耳草是一种贴地的爬藤草，英俗认为其汁能使儿童发育受阻。

332   **In her behalf that**：in behalf of her who.

335   **Never**：ever.

336   **aby**：pay penalty for. **holds**：cherishes.

338   **Of thine or mine, is most**：thine or mine, is greater.

339   **jole**：jowl, cheek.

340   **coil**：trouble. **'long of**：along of, on account of, caused by.

HELENA.   I will not trust you, I
No longer stay in your curst company.
Your hands than mine are quicker for a fray.
My legs are longer though, to run away.   [*Exit.*

345   HERMIA. I am amazed, and know not what to say.   [*Exit.*
OBERON. This is thy negligence: still thou mistakest,
Or else committ'st thy knaveries wilfully.
PUCK. Believe me, king of shadows, I mistook.
Did not you tell me I should know the man

350   By the Athenian garments be had on?
And so far blameless proves my enterprise,
That I have 'nointed an Athenian's eyes;
And so far am I glad it so did sort,
As this their jangling I esteem a sport.

355   OBERON. Thou see'st these lovers seek a place to fight:
Hie therefore, Robin, overcast the night;
The starry welkin cover thou anon
With drooping fog, as black as Acheron;
And lead these testy rivals so astray,

360   As one come not within another's way.
Like to Lysander sometime frame thy tongue,
Then stir Demetrius up with bitter wrong;
And sometime rail thou like Demetrius;
And from each other look thou lead them thus,

365   Till o'er their brows death-counterfeiting sleep
With leaden legs and batty wings doth creep:
Then crush this herb into Lysander's eye;
Whose liquor hath this virtuous property,
To take from thence all error with his might,

370   And make his eyeballs roll with wonted sight.
When they next wake, all this derision
Shall seem a dream and fruitless vision;
And back to Athens shall the lovers wend,
With league whose date till death shall never end.

346   **still**: always.
352   **'nointed**: anointed.
353   **sort**: fall out.
354   **As**: in that.
356   **Hie**: hasten.
357   **welkin**: sky.
358   **Acheron** [ˈækərɔn]：希腊神话中地狱里的黑河。
360   **As**: that.
361   Sometimes frame thy tongue like Lysander.
362   **wrong**: insult.
366   **batty**: bat-like.
368   **virtuous**: potent.、
369   **his might**: its power.
374   **league**: an alliance. **date**: duration.

375 Whiles I in this affair do thee employ,
I'll to my queen and beg her Indian boy;
And then I will her charmèd eye release
From monster's view, and all things shall be peace.

PUCK. My fairy lord, this must be done with haste,

380 For night's swift dragons cut the clouds full fast,
And yonder shines Aurora's harbinger;
At whose approach, ghosts, wandering here and
    there,
Troop home to churchyards: damned spirits all,
That in crossways and floods have burial,

385 Already to their wormy beds are gone;
For fear lest day should look their shames upon,
They wilfully themselves exile from light,
And must for aye consort with black-brow'd night.

OBERON. But we are spirits of another sort:

390 I with the morning's love have oft made sport;
And, like a forester, the groves may tread,
Even till the eastern gate, all fiery-red,
Opening on Neptune with fair blessed beams,
Turns into yellow gold his salt green streams.

395 But, notwithstanding, haste; make no delay:
We may effect this business yet ere day.   [*Exit.*

PUCK.   Up and down, up and down,
                   I will lead them up and down:
                   I am fear'd in field and town:

400   Goblin, lead them up and down.
Here comes one.

Re-enter LYSANDER.]

LYSANDER. Where art thou, proud Demetrius? speak thou
    now.

PUCK. Here, villain; drawn and ready. Where art thou?

LYSANDER. I will be with thee straight.

PUCK.   Follow me, then,

375 **Whiles**：while.

377 **charmèd**：bewitched.

378 **monster's**：前面省略冠词 the.

381 **Aurora's barbinger**：希腊神话中黎明女神 Aurora [ɔːrɔːrə]的先驱——晨星。

384 英俗自杀者不得葬在教堂墓地，只能葬在十字路口；溺死而未行葬礼者，其灵魂也受谴。

388 **for aye**：for ever.

390 I have often hunted with Aurora's lover Cephalus.

403 **drawn**：with sword drawn.

405   To plainer ground. [*Exit* LYSANDER, *as following the voice*.

    Re-enter DEMETRIUS.]

    DEMETRIUS.   Lysander! speak again:

    Thou runaway, thou coward, art thou fled?

    Speak! In some bush? Where dost thou hide thy head?

    PUCK. Thou coward, art thou bragging to the stars,

    Telling the bushes that thou look'st for wars,

410   And wilt not come? Come, recreant; come, thou child;

    I'll whip thee with a rod: he is defiled

    That draws a sword on thee.

    DEMETRIUS.   Yea, art thou there?

    PUCK. Follow my voice: we'll try no manhood here.

                          [*Exeunt*.

    Re-enter LYSANDER.]

    LYSANDER. He goes before me and still dares me on:

415   When I come where he calls, then he is gone.

    The villain is much lighter-heel'd than I:

    I follow'd fast, but faster he did fly;

    That fallen am I in dark uneven way,

    And here will rest me. [*Lies down*.] Come, thou gentle day!

420   For if but once thou show me thy gray light,

    I'll find Demetrius, and revenge this spite.   [*Sleeps*.

    Re-enter PUCK *and* DEMETRIUS.]

    PUCK. Ho, ho, ho! Coward, why comest thou not?

    DEMETRIUS. Abide me, if thou darest; for well I wot

    Thou runn'st before me, shifting every place,

425   And darest not stand, nor look me in the face.

    Where art thou now?

    PUCK.   Come hither: I am here.

    DEMETRIUS. Nay, then, thou mock'st me. Thou shalt buy this dear,

    If ever I thy face by daylight see:

404   **plainer**: more level.

418   **That**: with the result that.

423   **Abide**: wait for. **wot**: know.

427   **buy this dear**: pay dearly for this.

Now, go thy way. Faintness constraineth me
430   To measure out my length on this cold bed.
By day's approach look to be visited. [*Lies down
and sleeps.*

Re-enter HELENA.]

HELENA. O weary night, O long and tedious night,
Abate thy hour! Shine comforts from the east,
That I may back to Athens by daylight,
435   From these that my poor company detest:
And sleep, that sometimes shuts up sorrow's eye,
Steal me awhile from mine own company.

[*Lies down and sleeps.*

PUCK.   Yet but three? Come one more;
Two of both kinds make up four.
440   Here she comes, curst and sad:
Cupid is a knavish lad,
Thus to make poor females mad.

Re-enter HERMIA.]

HERMIA. Never so weary, never so in woe;
Bedabbled with the dew, and torn with briers;
445   I can no further crawl, no further go;
My legs can keep no pace with my desires.
Here will I rest me till the break of day.
Heavens shield Lysander, if they mean a fray!

[*Lies down and sleeps.*

PUCK.   On the ground
450   Sleep sound:
I'll apply
To your eye,
Gentle lover, remedy.

[*Squeezing the juice on* LYSANDER'S *eye.*

When thou wakest,
455   Thou takest
True delight

430　**measure out my lenght**：stretch out myself.

431　**look**：I expect.

433　**Abate**：shorten.

434　**That**：so that.

439　**Two…make**：数不一致，这种情况在当时偶有发生。

440　**curst**：cross.

In the sight
Of thy former lady's eye:
And the country proverb known,
460   That every man should take his own,
In your waking shall be shown:
Jack shall have Jill;
Nought shall go ill;
The man shall have his mare again, and all shall be
well.

[*Exit.*

462 Jack：普通男青年名；Jill：普通女青年名。这行是谚语。

464 这行也是谚语。

ACT IV

SCENE I

— The same.

LYSANDER, DEMETRIUS, HELENA, *and* HERMIA, *lying asleep.*

Enter TITANIA *and* BOTTOM; PEASEBLOSSOM, COBWEB, MOTH, MUSTARDSEED, *and other* FAIRIES *attending* OBERON *behind unseen.*

TITANIA. Come, sit thee down upon this flowery bed,
　　While I thy amiable cheeks do coy,
　　And stick musk-roses in thy sleek smooth head,
　　And kiss thy fair large ears, my gentle joy.

5　BOTTOM. Where's Peaseblossom?

PEASEBLOSSOM. Ready.

BOTTOM. Scratch my head, Peaseblossom. Where's Mounsieur Cobweb?

COBWEB. Ready.

BOTTOM. Mounsieur Cobweb, good mounsieur, get you your weapons in your hand, and kill me a red-
10　hipped humble-bee on the top of a thistle; and, good mounsieur, bring me the honey-bag. Do not fret yourself too much in the action, mounsieur; and, good mounsieur, have a care the honey-bag break not; I would be loath to have you overflown
15　with a honey-bag, signior. Where's Mounsieur Mustardseed?

MUSTARDSEED. Ready.

BOTTOM. Give me your neaf, Mounsieur Mustardseed. Pray you, leave your courtesy, good mounsieur.

MUSTARDSEED. What's your will?

20　BOTTOM. Nothing, good mounsieur, but to help Cava-

IV. i

    2 **coy**：caress.

    7 **Mounsieur**：Monsieur [məˈsjəː]，法语"先生"。

    15 **signior** [ˈsiːnjɔː]：意大利语"先生"。

    17 **neaf**：fist.

    20—21 **Cavalery**：Cavaliere，意大利语"骑士"。

lery Cobweb to scratch. I must to the barber's, mounsieur; for methinks I am marvelous hairy about the
face; and I am such a tender ass, if my hair do but
tickle me, I must scratch.

TITANIA. What, wilt thou hear some music, my sweet
love?

25 BOTTOM. I have a reasonable good ear in music. Let's have
the tongs and the bones.

TITANIA. Or say, sweet love, what thou desirest to eat.

BOTTOM. Truly, a peck of provender; I could munch
your good dry oats. Methinks I have a great desire
to a bottle of hay; good hay, sweet hay, hath no
30 fellow.

TITANIA. I have a venturous fairy that shall seek the
squirrel's hoard, and fetch thee new nuts.

BOTTOM. I had rather have a handful or two of dried peas.
But, I pray you, let none of your people stir me;
35 I have an exposition of sleep come upon me.

TITANIA. Sleep thou, and I will wind thee in my arms.
Fairies, be gone, and be all ways away. [*Exeunt*
FAIRIES.
So doth the woodbine the sweet honeysuckle
Gently entwist; the female ivy so
40 Enrings the barky fingers of the elm.
Oh, how I love thee! how I dote on thee!   [*They sleep.*
Enter PUCK.]

OBERON. [*Advancing*] Welcome, good Robin. See'st thou
this sweet sight?
Her dotage now I do begin to pity;
For, meeting her of late behind the wood,
45 Seeking sweet favors for this hateful fool,
I did upbraid her, and fall out with her;
For she his hairy temples then had rounded

26   **tongs and the bones**：火钳和骨制呱嗒板，最原始的乐器。

28   **peck**：干货体积量，相当于二加仑。**provender**：干饲料。

30   **bottle**：small bundle. **fellow**：equal，match.

35   **exposition**：应为 disposition，inclination.

36   **wind**：embrace.

37   **all ways**：in all directions.

38   **honeysuckle**：忍冬藤。

39   **ivy**：常春藤。

40   **Enrings**：encicles. **barky fingers**：branches. **elm**：榆树。

43   **dotage**：infatuation，excessive and silly love.

45   **favors**：flowers as love-tokens.

46   **fall out with**：quarrel with.

With coronet of fresh and fragrant flowers;
And that same dew, which sometime on the buds
50   Was wont to swell, like round and orient pearls,
Stood now within the pretty flowerets' eyes
Like tears, that did their own disgrace bewail.
When I had at my pleasure taunted her,
And she in mild terms begg'd my patience,
55   I then did ask of her her changeling child;
Which straight she gave me, and her fairy sent
To bear him to my bower in fairy land.
And now I have the boy, I will undo
This hateful imperfection of her eyes:
60   And, gentle Puck, take this transformed scalp
From off the head of this Athenian swain,
That, he awaking when the other do,
May all to Athens back again repair,
And think no more of this night's accidents,
65   But as the fierce vexation of a dream.
But first I will release the fairy queen.
     Be as thou wast wont to be;
     See as thou wast wont to see:
     Dian's bud o'er Cupid's flower
70   Hath such force and blessed power.
Now, my Titania; wake you, my sweet queen.
TITANIA. My Oberon! What visions have I seen!
Methought I was enamour'd of an ass.
OBERON. There lies your love.
75   TITANIA.   How came these things to pass?
O, how mine eyes do loathe his visage now!
OBERON. Silence awhile. Robin, take off this head.
Titania, music call; and strike more dead
Than common sleep of all these five the sense.
80   TITANIA. Music, ho! music, such as charmeth sleep!
                              [*Music, still.*

50   **orient**：① coming from the east；②lustrous.

57   **fairy land**：省略 the.

58   **now I**：now that I.

62   **That**：so that. **the other**：the others. 伊丽莎白时代常把 the other 看作集合名词。

63   **May all**：all may. **repair**：go.

65   **But as**：than. **fierce**：wild，extravagant.

69   **Dian's bud**：Diana's herb，月神草（学名叫 agnus castus，传说有保持贞操的效力，即上文 II. i 184 行和 III. ii 367 行所说的仙草）。

78—79   按自然字序，and 以后为 strike the sense of all these five (the four lovers and Bottom) more dead than common sleep.

80   **charmeth**：produces as by a charm.

PUCK. Now, when thou wakest, with thine own fool's
eyes peep.

OBERON. Sound, music! Come, my queen take hands
with me,

And rock the ground whereon these sleepers be.

Now thou and I are new in amity,

85 And will to-morrow midnight solemnly

Dance in Duke Theseus' house triumphantly,

And bless it to all fair prosperity:

There shall the pairs of faithful lovers be

Wedded, with Theseus, all in jollity.

90 PUCK.   Fairy king, attend, and mark:
            I do hear the morning lark.

OBERON.   Then, my queen, in silence sad,
            Trip we after night's shade:
            We the globe can compass soon,
            Swifter than the wandering moon.

TITANIA.   Come, my lord; and in our flight,
95   Tell me how it came this night,
            That I sleeping here was found
            With these mortals on the ground. [*Exeunt.*
                                [*Horns winded within.*

Enter THESEUS, HIPPOLYTA, EGEUS, *and train.*]

THESEUS. Go, one of you, find out the forester;

100 For now our observation is perform'd,

And since we have the vaward of the day,

My love shall hear the music of my hounds.

Uncouple in the western valley; let them go:

Dispatch, I say, and find the forester. [*Exit an*
      ATTENDANT.

105 We will, fair queen, up to the mountain's top,

And mark the musical confusion

Of hounds and echo in conjunction.

HIPPOLYTA. I was with Hercules and Cadmus once,

81　**thou**：对 Bottom 讲。

92　**sad**：sober，grave.

97　舞台说明 *winded*：sounded by blowing.

100　**now**：now that. **observation**：observance（of May day morning）.

101　**vaward**：vanguard，early part.

103　**Uncouple**：release the hounds（原是一对一对用链条拴住的）。

108　**Hercules** ['həːkjuliːz]：希腊神话中的大力英雄。**Cadmus** ['kædməs]：希腊神话中的英雄，Thebes 的创建人。

When in a wood of Crete they bay'd the bear

110   With hounds of Sparta: never did I hear

Such gallant chiding; for, besides the groves,

The skies, the fountains, every region near

Seem'd all one mutual cry: I never heard

So musical a discord, such sweet thunder.

115 THESEUS. My hounds are bred out of the Spartan kind,

So flew'd, so sanded; and their heads are hung

With ears that sweep away the morning dew;

Crook-knee'd, and dew-lapp'd like Thessalian bulls;

Slow in pursuit, but match'd in mouth like bells,

120   Each under each. A cry more tuneable

Was never holla'd to, nor cheer'd with horn,

In Crete, in Sparta, nor in Thessaly:

Judge when you hear. But, soft! what nymphs are
these?

EGEUS. My lord, this is my daughter here asleep;

125   And this, Lysander; this Demetrius is;

This Helena, old Nedar's Helena:

I wonder of their being here together.

THESEUS. No doubt they rose up early to observe

The rite of May; and, hearing our intent,

130   Came here in grace of our solemnity.

But speak, Egeus; is not this the day

That Hermia should give answer of her choice?

EGEUS. It is, my lord.

THESEUS. Go, bid the huntsmen awake them with their
horns.

    [*Horns and shout within*. LYSANDER, DEMETRIUS,
      HELENA, *and* HERMIA *wake and start up*.

135   Good morrow, friends. Saint Valentine is past:

Begin these wood-birds but to couple now?

LYSANDER. Pardon, my lord.

THESEUS.   I pray you all, stand up.

109   **Crete** [kriːt]：地中海东部克里特岛。**bay'd**：brought to bay.

110   **Sparta** [ˈspɑːtə]：斯巴达,古希腊城邦之一,产猎狗。

111   **childing**：barking.

116   **flew'd**：狗的上唇两旁有大块下垂皮肉的(这样的猎狗嘴特大)。**sanded**：沙色的。

118   **Thessalian** [θeˈseiljən]：希腊东北部 Thessaly 地区的。

120   **Each under each**：一只比一只小(一套从大到小的钟,喻猎狗的叫声从低音到高音各不相同,而配成一套)。**cry**：pack of hounds.

123   **soft**：stay, stop.

127   **of**：at.

130   **in grace of**：in honor of. **solemnity**：festivity.

132   **That**：when.

135   **Saint Valentine** [ˈvæləntain]：传说在 Saint Valentine's Day,即 2 月 14 日。鸟雀选择配偶,因此男女青年也在这天选择对象。

136   **but**：only — Do these wood-birds begin to couple only now?

I know you two are rival enemies:
How comes this gentle concord in the world,
140   That hatred is so far from jealousy,
To sleep by hate, and fear no enmity?
LYSANDER. My lord, I shall reply amazedly,
Half sleep, half waking: but as yet, I swear,
I cannot truly say how I came here;
145   But, as I think, — for truly would I speak,
And now I do bethink me, so it is, —
I came with Hermia hither: our intent
Was to be gone from Athens, where we might,
Without the peril of the Athenian law...
150   EGEUS. Enough, enough, my lord; you have enough:
I beg the law, the law, upon his head.
They would have stolen away; they would, Demetrius,
Thereby to have defeated you and me,
You of your wife and me of my consent,
155   Of my consent that she should be your wife.
DEMETRIUS. My lord, fair Helen told me of their
stealth,
Of this their purpose hither to this wood;
And I in fury hither follow'd them,
Fair Helena in fancy following me.
160   But, my good lord, I wot not by what power, —
But by some power it is, — my love to Hermia,
Melted as the snow, seems to me now
As the remembrance of an idle gaud,
Which in my childhood I did dote upon;
165   And all the faith, the virtue of my heart,
The object and the pleasure of mine eye,
Is only Helena. To her, my lord,
Was I betroth'd ere I saw Hermia:
But, like in sickness, did I loath this food;
170   But, as in health, come to my natural taste,

140 **jealousy**: suspicion.

141 **To**: as to. **by hate**: beside hated people.

146 **bethink me**: stop to think.

148 **where**: to a place where.

149 Beyond the dangerous reach of the Athenian law.

153 **defeated**: defrauded.

160 **wot**: know.

163 **idle gaud**: worthless toy, trinket.

        Now I do wish it, love it, long for it,

        And will for evermore be true to it.

      THESEUS. Fair lovers, you are fortunately met:

        Of this discourse we more will hear anon.

175   Egeus, I will overbear your will;

        For in the temple, by and by, with us

        These couples shall eternally be knit:

        And, for the morning now is something worn,

        Our purposed hunting shall be set aside.

180   Away with us to Athens! three and three,

        We'll hold a feast in great solemnity.

        Come, Hippolyta. [*Exeunt* THESEUS, HIPPOLYTA, *and*
          train.

      DEMETRIUS. These things seem small and undistingui-
        shable,

        Like far-off mountains turned into clouds.

185 HERMIA. Methinks I see these things with parted eye,

        When every thing seems double.

      HELENA.   So methinks:

        And I have found Demetrius like a jewel,

        Mine own, and not mine own.

      DEMETRIUS.   Are you sure

        That we are awake? It seems to me

190   That yet we sleep, we dream. Do not you think

        The Duke was here, and bid us follow him?

      HERMIA. Yea; and my father.

      HELENA.   And Hippolyta.

      LYSANDER. And he did bid us follow to the temple.

      DEMETRIUS. Why, then, we are awake: let's follow him;

195   And by the way let us recount our dreams.[*Exeunt*.

      BOTTOM. [*Awaking*] When my cue comes, call me, and

        I will answer: my next is, 'Most fair Pyramus.' High-

        ho! Peter Quince! Flute, the bellows-mender! Snout,

        the tinker! Starveling! God's my life, stolen

175　**overbear**：prevail over.

180　**three and three**：三人一组，是分列式转向时的口号，跳舞也有三人一组的。

185　**parted eye**：divided eyes.

198—199　**God's my life**：赌咒词。**stolen hence**：they have left stealthily.

hence, and left me asleep! I have had a most rare
200   vision. I have had a dream, past the wit of a man to
say what dream it was: man is but an ass, if he go
about to expound this dream. Methought I was —
there is no man can tell what. Methought I was, —
and methought I had, — but man is but a patched
205   fool, if he will offer to say what methought I had.
The eye of man hath not heard, the ear of man
hath not seen, man's hand is not able to taste, his
tongue to conceive, nor his heart to report, what
my dream was. I will get Peter Quince to write
210   a ballad of this dream: it shall be called Bottom's
Dream, because it hath no bottom; and I will sing it in
the latter end of a play, before the Duke: peradven-
ture, to make it the more gracious, I shall sing it at
her death.   [*Exit.*

SCENE II

Athens. QUINCE'S *house.*

Enter QUINCE, FLUTE, SNOUT, *and* STARVELING.]

QUINCE. Have you sent to Bottom's house? Is he come
home yet?

STARVELING. He cannot be heard of. Out of doubt he is
transported.

FLUTE. If he come not, then the play is marred: it goes
not forward, doth it?

5   QUINCE. It is not possible: you have not a man in all
Athens able to discharge Pyramus but he.

FLUTE. No, he hath simply the best wit of any handicraft
man in Athens.

QUINCE. Yea , and the best person too; and he is a very
10   paramour for a sweet voice.

FLUTE. You must say ' paragon ' : a paramour is , God

201—202 go about: try.

204—205 patched fool: clown wearing a patchwork costume.

211 hath no bottom: is unfathomable.

214 her: 不知指谁，可能指 Thisbe.

IV. ii

2 transported: carried off (by the fairies).

3—4 it goes not forward: it is not making progress.

6 discharge: perform.

7—8 wit: intellect. **best wit of any handicraft man**: best wit of all handicraftsmen.

9 person: figure, appearance.

10 paramour: illicit lover of a married man or woman.

bless us, a thing of naught.

Enter SNUG.]

SNUG. Masters, the Duke is coming from the temple, and there is two or three lords and ladies more married: if our sport had gone forward we had all
15   been made men.

FLUTE. O sweet bully Bottom! Thus hath he lost six-pence a day during his life; he could not have 'scaped sixpence a day: an the Duke had not given him sixpence a day for playing Pyramus, I'll be hanged; he would have deserved it: sixpence a day in Pyramus,
20   or nothing.

Enter BOTTOM.]

BOTTOM. Where are these lads? where are these hearts?

QUINCE. Bottom! O most courageous day! O most happy hour!

BOTTOM. Masters, I am to discourse wonders: but ask me not what; for if I tell you, I am no true Athenian.
25   I will tell you every thing, right as it fell out.

QUINCE. Let us hear, sweet Bottom.

BOTTOM. Not a word of me. All that I will tell you is, that the Duke hath dined. Get your apparel together, good strings to your beards, new ribbons to your pumps; meet presently at the palace; every man
30   look o'er his part; for the short and the long is, our play is preferred. In any case, let Thisby have clean linen; and let not him that plays the lion pair his nails, for they shall hang out for the lion's claws. And, most dear actors, eat no onions nor garlic, for we are to utter sweet breath ; and I do not
35   doubt but to hear them say, it is a sweet comedy. No more words: away! go, away!

                                                    [*Exeunt.*

11   **thing of maught**：something evil.

13   **there is**：先单数谓语，后复数主语，当时常见。

14—15   **we had all been made men**：our fortunes would have been made.

22   **courageous**：似是 Quince 用错的字，他可能想说 auspicious.

23   **I am to**：I am ready to.

27   **of**：from.

29   **pumps**：当时上流社会流行的一种浅鞋，前面缀以缎结。

31   **preferred**：recommended，put forward.

ACT V

SCENE I

Athens. The palace of THESEUS.

Enter THESEUS, HIPPOLYTA, PHILOSTRATE, LORDS, *and*
    ATTENDANTS.]

HIPPOLYTA.'Tis strange, my Theseus, that these lovers
    speak of.

THESEUS.More strange than true: I never may believe
    These antique fables, nor these fairy toys.
    Lovers and madmen have such seething brains,
5   Such shaping fantasies, that apprehend
    More than cool reason ever comprehends.
    The lunatic, the lover and the poet
    Are of imagination all compact:
    One sees more devils than vast hell can hold,
10   That is, the madman: the lover, all as frantic,
    Sees Helen's beauty in a brow of Egypt:
    The poet's eye, in a fine frenzy rolling,
    Doth glance from heaven to earth, from earth to
      heaven;
    And as imagination bodies forth
15   The forms of things unknown, the poet's pen
    Turns them to shapes, and gives to airy nothing
    A local habitation and a name.
    Such tricks hath strong imagination,
    That, if it would but apprehend some joy,
20   It comprehends some bringer of that joy;
    Or in the night, imagining some fear,
    How easy is a bush supposed a bear!

HIPPOLYTA. But all the story of the night told over,
    And all their minds transfigured so together,

V. i

   1   **that**：what.

   2   **may**：can.

   3   **antique**：grotesque. **fairy toys**：idle tales about fairies.

   8   **compact**：composed.

   11   **Helen**：海伦是希腊神话中的美人，就是因为抢夺她，引起了 Troy 的战争。**Egypt**：gypsy，吉卜赛人，皮肤黝黑。**a brow of Egypt**：the face of a gypsy.

   21   **imagining**：if one imagines.

25   More witnesseth than fancy's images,
      And grows to something of great constancy;
      But, howsoever, strange and admirable.

THESEUS. Here come the lovers, full of joy and mirth.

Enter LYSANDER, DEMETRIUS, HERMIA, *and* HELENA.]

      Joy, gentle friends! joy and fresh days of love
      Accompany your hearts!

30 LYSANDER.   More than to us
      Wait in your royal walks, your board, your bed!

THESEUS. Come now; what masques, what dances
      shall we have,
      To wear away this long age of three hours
      Between our after-supper and bed-time?

35   Where is our usual manager of mirth?
      What revels are in hand? Is there no play,
      To ease the anguish of a torturing hour?
      Call Philostrate.

PHILOSTRATE.   Here, mighty Theseus.

THESEUS. Say, what abridgment have you for this
      evening?

40   What masque? what music? How shall we beguile
      The lazy time, if not with some delight?

PHILOSTRATE. There is a brief how many sports are
ripe:
      Make choice of which your highness will see first.

                             [*Giving a paper.*

THESEUS.[*Reads*] The battle with the Centaurs, to
      be sung

45   By an Athenian eunuch to the harp.
      We'll none of that: that have I told my love,
      In glory of my kinsman Hercules.
      [*Reads*] The riot of the tipsy Bacchanals,
      Tearing the Thracian singer in their rage.

50   That is an old device; and it was play'd

25 gives evidence of more than the creations of the imagination.

27 **howsoever**: howsoever it may be, in any case. **admirable**: to be wondered at.

30 **More than to us**: more people than us.

31 **Wait in your**: may they (joy and fresh days of love) attend your.

32 **masques**: amateur dramatic and musical entertainments, originally in dumb show, later with metrical dialogue.

34 **after-supper**: dessert of fruits and sweetmeats after supper dishes.

39 **abridgment**: means of shortening thd time, pastime.

42 Here is a short account of how many entertainments are ready.

43 **of**：按现代语法为多余。

44 **Centaurs** ['sentɔːz]：希腊神话中上身为人,下身为马的神怪。

48 **Bacchanals** ['bækənəlz]：希腊神话中酒神 Bacchus 的祭司和信徒。

49 **Thracian** ['θreiʃjən] **singer**：希腊神话中色雷斯诗人 Orpheus ['ɔːfjuːs]因失妻不断哀歌,惹怒了醉酒的妇女,被撕成碎片。

50 **device**: show.

When I from Thebes came last a conqueror.
[*Reads*] The thrice three Muses mourning for the death
Of Learning, late deceased in beggary.
That is some satire, keen and critical,
55   Not sorting with a nuptial ceremony.
[*Reads*] A tedious brief scene of young Pyramus
And his love Thisbe; very tragical mirth.
Merry and tragical! tedious and brief!
That is, hot ice and wondrous strange snow.
60   How shall we find the concord of this discord?
PHILOSTRATE. A play there is, my lord, some ten
    words long,
    Which is as brief as I have known a play;
    But by ten words, my lord, it is too long,
    Which makes it tedious; for in all the play
65   There is not one word apt, one player fitted:
    And tragical, my noble lord, it is;
    For Pyramus therein doth kill himself,
    Which, when I saw rehearsed, I must confess,
    Made mine eyes water; but more merry tears
70   The passion of loud laughter never shed.
THESEUS. What are they that do play it?
PHILOSTRATE. Hard-handed men, that work in Athens
    here,
    Which never labor'd in their minds till now;
    And now have toil'd their unbreathed memories
75   With this same play, against your nuptial.
THESEUS. And we will hear it.
PHILOSTRATE.   No, my noble lord;
    It is not for you: I have heard it over,
    And it is nothing, nothing in the world;
    Unless you can find sport in their intents,
80   Extremely stretch'd and conn'd with cruel pain,
    To do you service.

52   **thrice three Muses** ['mjuːziz]：希腊神话中司文艺的九位女神。

54   **keen**：sharp.

55   **sorting with**：befitting.

70   **passion**：strong feeling.

73   **Which**：who（伊丽莎白时代关系代词的分工还不明确）。

74   **unbreathed**：unexercised.

75   **against**：in preparation for.

76   答复用 And 开头，有强调肯定之义。此句相当于 That is exactly what we will hear.

79   **intents**：purposes，desires.

80   **conn'd**：learnt by heart. **pain**：labor，effort.

THESEUS.　　　　I will hear that play;
　　For never any thing can be amiss,
　　When simpleness and duty tender it.
　　Go, bring them in; and take your places, ladies.

　　　　　　　　　　　　　　　[*Exit* PHILOSTRATE.

85　HIPPOLYTA. I love not to see wretchedness o'ercharged,
　　And duty in his service perishing.
　　THESEUS. Why, gentle sweet, you shall see no such thing.
　　HIPPOLYTA. He says they can do nothing in this kind.
　　THESEUS. The kinder we, to give them thanks for nothing.

90　　Our sport shall be to take what they mistake:
　　And what poor duty cannot do, noble respect
　　Takes it in might, not merit.
　　Where I have come, great clerks have purposed
　　To greet me with premeditated welcomes;

95　　Where I have seen them shiver and look pale,
　　Make periods in the midst of sentences,
　　Throttle their practiced accent in their fears,
　　And, in conclusion, dumbly have broke off,
　　Not paying me a welcome. Trust me, sweet,

100　　Out of this silence yet I picked a welcome;
　　And in the modesty of fearful duty
　　I read as much as from the rattling tongue
　　Of saucy and audacious eloquence.
　　Love, therefore, and tongue-tied simplicity

105　　In least speak most, to my capacity.
　　Re-enter PHILOSTRATE.]

　　PHILOSTRATE. So please your grace, the Prologue is
　　　　address'd.

　　THESEUS. Let him approach.　　[*Flourish of trumpets.*
　　Enter QUINCE *for the Prologue.*]

　　PROLOGUE. If we offend, it is with our good will.
　　　　That you should think, we come not to offend,

110　　But with good will. To show our simple skill,

85   **wretchedness**：the lowly in both social position and intellect.

91   **respect**：consideration.

92   **might**：the great effort made.

93   **clerks**：scholars.

94   **welcomes**：welcoming speeches.

98   they 省略，后半句等于说 they have broken off dumbly.

104   **simplicity**：artlessness.

105   **to my capacity**：as far as I am able to understand.

106   **address'd**：prepared.

108—117   这段开场白的诗体是缺少前四行的十四行诗，中间句读故意错误，以引人发笑。

That is the true beginning of our end.
Consider then, we come but in despite.
   We do not come, as minding to content you,
Our true intent is. All for your delight,
115   We are not here. That you should here repent you,
   The actors are at hand; and, by their show,
   You shall know all, that you are like to know.
THESEUS. This fellow doth not stand upon points.
LYSANDER. He hath rid his prologue like a rough colt; he
120   knows not the stop. A good moral, my lord: it is not
    enough to speak, but to speak true.
HIPPOLYTA. Indeed he hath played on his prologue like a
child on a recorder; a sound, but not in govern-
ment.
THESEUS. His speech was like a tangled chain; nothing
125   impaired, but all disordered. Who is next?

Enter PYRAMUS *and* THISBE, WALL, MOONSHINE, *and* LION.]
PROLOGUE. Gentles, perchance you wonder at this show;
   But wonder on, till truth make all things plain.
   This man is Pyramus, if you would know;
   This beauteous lady Thisby is certain.
130   This man, with lime and rough-cast, doth present
   Wall, that vile Wall which did these lovers sunder;
And through Wall's chink, poor souls, they are content
   To whisper. At the which let no man wonder.
This man, with lanthorn, dog, and bush of thorn,
135   Presenteth Moonshine; for, if you will know,
By moonshine did these lovers think no scorn
   To meet at Ninus' tomb, there, there to woo.
This grisly beast, which Lion hight by name,
   The trusty Thisby, coming first by night,
140   Did scare away, or rather did affright;
   And, as she fled, her mantle she did fall,
   Which Lion vile with bloody mouth did stain.

112   **in despite**：in defiance of another's wish.

116,126   **show**：演员的亮相。

118   **stand upon points**：be particular about marks of punctuation.

119   **rid**：ridden.

123   **government**：control.

136   **did…think no scorn**：did not regard as disgraceful.

138   **hight**：called.

141   **fall**：drop(不及物动词用作及物)。

Anon comes Pyramus, sweet youth and tall,

And finds his trusty Thisby's mantle slain:

145 Whereat, with blade, with bloody blameful blade,

He bravely broach'd his boiling bloody breast:

And Thisby, tarrying in mulberry shade,

His dagger drew, and died. For all the rest,

Let Lion, Moonshine, Wall, and lovers twain

150 At large discourse, while here they do remain.

[*Exeunt* PROLOGUE, PYRAMUS, THISBE, LION,

and MOONSHINE.

THESEUS. I wonder if the lion be to speak.

DEMETRIUS. No wonder, my lord: one lion may, when many asses do.

WALL. In this same interlude it doth befall

155 That I, one Snout by name, present a wall;

And such a wall, as I would have you think,

That had in it a crannied hole or chink,

Through which the lovers, Pyramus and Thisby,

Did whisper often very secretly.

160 This loam, this rough-cast, and this stone, doth show

That I am that same wall; the truth is so:

And this the cranny is, right and sinister,

Through which the fearful lovers are to whisper.

THESEUS. Would you desire lime and hair to speak better?

165 DEMETRIUS. It is the wittiest partition that ever I heard discourse, my lord.

THESEUS. Pyramus draws near the wall: silence!

Re-enter PYRAMUS.]

PYRAMUS. O grim-look'd night! O night with hue so black!

O night, which ever art when day is not!

170 O night, O night! alack, alack, alack,

143   tall：goodly，fine.

145—146　这里莎士比亚故意用许多头韵，以起到模拟夸张的滑稽作用。前后名词缺冠词的现象较多，也是他嘲弄的文体，不是正规。

149   lovers twain：the two lovers.

150   At large：at length.

151   be to speak：would speak.

162   right and sinister：right and left，horizontal.

165   wittiest：most intelligent. **partition**：① wall；② section of a speech.

168   grim-look'd：这里用 look 的过去分词不寻常，一般用现在分词 looking.

I fear my Thisby's promise is forgot!

And thou, O wall, O sweet, O lovely wall,

That stand'st between her father's ground and mine!

Thou wall, O wall, O sweet and lovely wall,

175   Show me thy chink, to blink through with mine eyne!

                          [WALL *holds up his fingers.*

Thanks, courteous wall: Jove shield thee well for this!

But what see I? No Thisby do I see.

O wicked wall, through whom I see no bliss!

Cursed be thy stones for thus deceiving me!

180 THESEUS. The wall, methinks, being sensible, should curse again.

PYRAMUS. No, in truth, sir, he should not. 'Deceiving me' is Thisby's cue: she is to enter now, and I am to spy her through the wall. You shall see, it will fall pat as I told you.

185   Yonder she comes.

Re-enter THISBE.]

THISBE. O wall, full often hast thou heard my moans,

    For parting my fair Pyramus and me!

My cherry lips have often kiss'd thy stones,

    Thy stones with lime and hair knit up in thee.

190 PYRAMUS. I see a voice: now will I to the chink,

To spy an I can hear my Thisby's face.

Thisby!

THISBE. My love thou art, my love I think.

PYRAMUS. Think what thou wilt, I am thy lover's grace;

    And, like Limander, am I trusty still.

195 THISBE. And I like Helen, till the Fates me kill.

PYRAMUS. Not Shafalus to Procrus was so true.

THISBE. As Shafalus to Procrus, I to you.

PYRAMUS. O, kiss me through the hole of this vile wall!

THISBE. I kiss the wall's hole, not your lips at all.

171   **forgot**：forgotten（旧时的过去分词形式）。

180   **sensible**：有知觉的。

181   **again**：back，in return.

184   **fall**：happen. **pat**：precisely.

191   **spy**：look. 这里故意将视觉和听觉相混，达到滑稽的目的。
an：if.

193   **grace**：本来 your grace 是一种尊称，类似"阁下"；这里称 thy
lover's grace，有如说"你的爱人阁下"，是滑稽的称呼。

194   **Limander**：可能是 Leander 的错读，他是希腊神话中忠诚的
爱人，每夜游过海峡去见 Hero，后溺死。

196   **Shafalus** 和 **Procrus**：是 Cephalus 和 Procris 的错读，这两夫
妻据希腊神话因女方变心而生分，最后男的误杀女的，又复自杀，死前
两人和好。

PYRAMUS. Wilt thou at Ninny's tomb meet me
200   straightway?

THISBE. 'Tide life, 'tide death, I come without delay.

                          [*Exeunt* PYRAMUS *and* THISBE.

WALL. Thus have I, wall, my part discharged so;
    And, being done, thus wall away doth go.   [*Exit.*

THESEUS. Now is the mural down between the two neigh-
    bors.

205   DEMETRIUS. No remedy, my lord, when walls are so will-
    ful to hear without warning.

HIPPOLYTA. This is the silliest stuff that ever I heard.

THESEUS. The best in this kind are but shadows; and the
    worst are no worse, if imagination amend them.

210   HIPPOLYTA. It must be your imagination then, and not
    theirs.

THESEUS. If we imagine no worse of them than they of
    themselves, they may pass for excellent men. Here come
    two noble beasts in, a man and a lion.

Re-enter LION *and* MOONSHINE.]

LION. You, ladies, you, whose gentle hearts do fear
215   The smallest monstrous mouse that creeps on floor,
    May now perchance both quake and tremble here,
        When lion rough in wildest rage doth roar,
    Then know that I, one Snug the joiner, am
    A lion-fell, nor else no lion's dam;
220   For, if I should as lion come in strife
    Into this place, 'twere pity on my life.

THESEUS. A very gentle beast, and of a good conscience.

DEMETRIUS. The very best at a beast, my lord, that e'er
    I saw.

LYSANDER. This lion is a very fox for his valor.

225   THESEUS. True; and a goose for his discretion.

DEMETRIUS. Not so, my lord; for his valor cannot carry
    his discretion; and the fox carries the goose.

201　'Tide：betide，come.

208　this kind：指 the actors.

219　lion-fell：fierce lion. dam：dame，wife.

224　fox：狐狸狡猾，但胆小。his：its.

225　goose：以傻笨著名。

THESEUS. His discretion, I am sure, cannot carry his valor; for the goose carries not the fox. It is well: leave it to his discretion, and let us listen to the
230   moon.

MOON. This lanthorn doth the hornèd moon present; —

DEMETRIUS. He should have worn the horns on his head.

THESEUS. He is no crescent, and his horns are invisible within the circumference.

235   MOON. This lanthorn doth the horned moon present;
Myself the man i' the moon do seem to be.

THESEUS. This is the greatest error of all the rest: the man should be put into the lantern. How is it else the man i' the moon?

240   DEMETRIUS. He dares not come there for the candle; for, you see, it is already in snuff.

HIPPOLYTA. I am aweary of this moon: would he would change!

THESEUS. It appears, by his small light of discretion,
245   that he is in the wane; but yet, in courtesy, in all reason, we must stay the time.

LYSANDER. Proceed, Moon.

MOON. All that I have to say, is, to tell you that the lanthorn is the moon; I, the man i'teh moon; this
250   thorn-bush, my thorn-bush; and this dog, my dog.

DEMETRIUS. Why, all these should be in the lantern; for all these are in the moon. But, silence! here comes Thisbe.

Re-enter THISBE.]

THISBE. This is old Ninny's tomb. Where is my love?

LION. [*Roaring*] Oh—   [THISBE *runs off*.
255   DEMETRIUS. Well roared, Lion.

THESEUS. Well run, Thisbe.

HIPPOLYTA. Well shone, Moon. Truly, the moon shines

231   **lanthorn**：lantern，此处读作 lant-horn，和下文 horned，horns 配成文字游戏。**hornèd moon**：长了角的月亮，新月。

232   **horns on his head**：头上长角是老婆偷人的象征。

237   **两种最高级说法的混合**：the greatest of all 和 greater than all the rest.

240   **for**：for fear of.

241   **in snuff**：in need of snuffing.

with a good grace.

       [*The* LION *shakes* THISBE'S *mantle*, *and exit.*

THESEUS. Well moused, Lion.

260 DEMETRIUS. And then came Pyramus.

LYSANDER. And so the lion vanished.

Re-enter PYRAMUS.]

PYRAMUS. Sweet Moon, I thank thee for thy sunny
    beams;

    I thank thee, Moon, for shining now so bright;

    For, by thy gracious, golden, glittering gleams,

265   I trust to take of truest Thisby sight.

        But stay, O spite!

        But mark, poor knight,

    What dreadful dole is here!

        Eyes, do you see?

270   How can it be?

    O dainty duck! O dear!

        Thy mantle good,

          What, stain'd with blood!

    Approach, ye Furies fell!

275   O Fates, come, come,

        Cut thread and thrum;

    Quail, crush, conclude, and quell!

THESEUS. This passion, and the death of a dear friend,
    would go near to make a man look sad.

280 HIPPOLYTA. Beshrew my heart, but I pity the man.

PYRAMUS. O wherefore, Nature, didst thou lions frame?

    Since lion vile hath here deflower'd my dear;

    Which is—no, no—which was the fairest dame

      That lived, that loved, that liked, that look'd with
      cheer.

285   Come, tears, confound;

      Out, sword, and wound

    The pap of Pyramus;

259　**moused**：tore，bit.

268　**dole**：cause of grief.

274　**Furies**：希腊神话中的复仇三女神。

275　**Fates**：希腊神话中的司命运三女神：其一执纺锤，其二织人的生命之网，其三用剪割断网线。

276　**thread**：经线。**thrum**：线头。**thread and thrum**：good and bad together.

277　**Quail**：overpower. **quell**：kill.

278　**passion**：suffering.

280　**Beshrew**：the devil take.

282　**deflower'd**：ravaged.

283　**which**：who.

287　**pap**：nipple.

Ay, that left pap,

Where heart doth hop: [*Stabs himself.*

290 Thus die I, thus, thus, thus.

Now am I dead;

Now am I fled

My soul is in the sky:

Tongue, lose thy light;

295 Moon, take thy flight: [*Exit* MOONSHINE.

Now die, die, die, die, die.   [*Dies.*

DEMETRIUS. No die, but an ace, for him; for he is but one.

LYSANDER. Less than an ace, man; for he is dead; he is nothing.

THESEUS. With the help of a surgeon he might yet
300   recover, and prove an ass.

HIPPOLYTA. How chance Moonshine is gone before Thisbe comes back and finds her lover?

THESEUS. She will find him by starlight. Here she comes; and her passion ends the play.

Re-enter THISBE.]

305 HIPPOLYTA. Methinks she should not use a long one for such a Pyramus: I hope she will be brief.

DEMETRIUS. A mote will turn the balance, which Pyramus, which Thisbe, is the better; he for a man, God warrant us; she for a woman, God bless us.

310 LYSANDER. She hath spied him already with those sweet eyes.

DEMETRIUS. And thus she means, videlicet: —

THISBE.   Asleep, my love?

What, dead, my dove?

O Pyramus, arise!

315   Speak, speak. Quite dumb?

Dead, dead? A tomb

Must cover thy sweet eyes.

297   die：one of a pair of dice，单颗骰子。**ace**：a single spot on a die；ace 和 ass 读音近似。

301   How chance：how may it chance（happen）that.

304   passion：① suffering and death；② passionate speech.

307—308   mote：minute particle. **which** … , **which**：whether … or

311   means：①〔英国北部方言〕laments；②〔法律〕lodges a complaint. **videlicet**〔拉丁语，viˈdiːliset〕：you may see.

These lily lips,

This cherry nose,

320   These yellow cowslip cheeks,

Are gone, are gone:

Lovers, make moan:

His eyes were green as leeks.

O Sisters Three,

325   Come, come to me,

With hands as pale as milk;

Lay them in gore,

Since you have shore

With shears his thread of silk.

330   Tongue, not a word:

Come, trusty sword;

Come, blade, my breast imbrue: [*Stabs herself.*

And, fare well, friends;

Thus Thisbe ends:

335   Adieu, adieu, adieu.   [*Dies.*

THESEUS. Moonshine and Lion are left to bury the dead.

DEMETRIUS. Ay, and Wall too.

BOTTOM. [*Starting up*] No, I assure you; the wall is
down that parted their fathers. Will it please you to see
340   the epilogue, or to hear a Bergomask dance between
two of our company?

THESEUS. No epilogue, I pray you; for your play needs no
excuse. Never excuse; for when the players are
all dead, there need none to be blamed. Marry, if
he that writ it had played Pyramus and hanged
345   himself in Thisbe's garter, it would have been a fine
tragedy: and so it is, truly; and very notably discharged. But, come, your Bergomask: let your
epilogue alone.   [*A dance.*

The iron tongue of midnight hath told twelve:

Lovers, to bed, 'tis almost fairy time.

324 **Sisters Three**：the Fates. 见上 275 行。

328 **shore**：应为 shorn，为凑韵而说 shore.

332 **imbrue**：pierce.

340 **Bergomask dance**：a rustic dance after the manner of Bergamo，in Italy.

344 **writ**：wrote.

348 **iron tongue**：指钟舌。

350 I fear we shall out-sleep the coming morn,
As much as we this night have overwatch'd.
This palpable-gross play hath well beguiled
The heavy gait of night. Sweet friends, to bed.
A fortnight hold we this solemnity,
355 In nightly revels and new jollity.   [*Exeunt.*
Enter PUCK.]
PUCK. Now the hungry lion roars,
    And the wolf behowls the moon;
Whilst the heavy ploughman snores,
    All with weary task fordone.
360 Now the wasted brands do glow,
    Whilst the screech-owl, screeching loud,
Puts the wretch that lies in woe
    In remembrance of a shroud.
Now it is the time of night,
365   That the graves, all gaping wide,
Every one lets forth his sprite,
    In the church-way paths to glide:
And we fairies, that do run
    By the triple Hecate's team,
370 From the presence of the sun,
    Following darkness like a dream,
Now are frolic; not a mouse
Shall disturb this hallow'd house:
I am sent with broom before,
375 To sweep the dust behind the door.
Enter OBERON *and* TITANIA *with their train.*]
OBERON. Through the house give gimmering light,
    By the dead and drowsy fire:
Every elf and fairy sprite
    Hop as light as bird from brier;
And this ditty, after me,
380 Sing, and dance it trippingly.

351 **overwatch'd**：stayed up too late.

352 **palpable-gross**：obviously crude.

357 **behowls**：howls against.

358 **heavy**：weary.

359 **fordone**：exhausted.

360 **wasted**：burnt-out.

366 **his**：its. **sprite**：spirit，ghost.

369 **triple Hecate** ['hekəti]：三重身份的女神，在天上、地狱和地上有不同的名字；这里视她为月亮和黑夜的女神。

372 **frolic**：frolicsome，merry.

380 **it**：泛指，这里等于说 the dance.

TITANIA. First, rehearse your song by rote,
    To each word a warbling note;
    Hand in hand, with fairy grace,
    Will we sing, and bless this place.   [*Song and
                                                        dance.*

385 OBERON. Now, until the break of day,
    Through this house each fairy stray.
    To the best bride-bed will we,
    Which by us shall blessed be;
    And the issue there create
390   Ever shall be fortunate.
    So shall all the couples three
    Ever true in loving be;
    And the blots of Nature's hand
    Shall not in their issue stand;
395   Never mole, hare lip, nor scar,
    Nor mark prodigious, such as are
    Despised in nativity,
    Shall upon their children be.
    With this field-dew consecrate,
400   Every fairy take his gait;
    And each several chamber bless,
    Through this palace, with sweet peace,
    Ever shall in safety rest,
    And the owner of it blest.
405   Trip away; make no stay;
    Meet me all by break of day.
                        [*Exeunt* OBERON, TITANIA, *and train.*
    PUCK. If we shadows have offended,
    Think but this, and all is mended,
    That you have but slumber'd here,
410   While these visions did appear.
    And this weak and idle theme,
    No more yielding but a dream,

381 **rehearse… by rote**: repeat from memory.

387 **will we**: will we go.

389 **issue**：女子，后嗣。**create**：created 过去分词的标志 d 在 t 音后常省略，399 行 consecrate 同。

396 **mark prodigious**：ominous birthmark.

399 **consecrate**：consecrated，blessed.

400 **take his gait**：take his way.

401 **several**：separate.

407—422 这是一段收场白，是 Puck 直接对观众说的话。

412 Yielding no more than a dream.

Gentles, do not reprehend:
If you pardon, we will mend.
415   And, as I am an honest Puck,
If we have unearned luck
Now to 'scape the serpent's tongue,
We will make amends ere long;
Else the Puck a liar call:
420   So, good night unto you all.
Give me your hands, if we be friends,
And Robin shall restore amends.   [*Exit.*

413 **Gentles**: gentlefolk. **reprehend**: rebuke, blame.

417 **serpent's tongue**: hissing (from the audience).

421 **hands**: applause.

图书在版编目(CIP)数据

仲夏夜之梦 /(英)莎士比亚(Shakespeare,W.)著;
裘克安注释.—北京:商务印书馆,2014(2016.3 重印)
(莎翁戏剧经典)
ISBN 978-7 -100-09899-1

Ⅰ.①仲… Ⅱ.①莎… ②裘… Ⅲ.①英语—语言
读物 ②剧本—英国—中世纪 Ⅳ.①H319.4;I

中国版本图书馆 CIP 数据核字(2013)第 072182 号

所有权利保留。

未经许可,不得以任何方式使用。

莎翁戏剧经典
ZHÒNGXIÀYÈ ZHĪ MÈNG
仲 夏 夜 之 梦
〔英〕威廉·莎士比亚 著

裘克安 注释

商 务 印 书 馆 出 版
(北京王府井大街36号 邮政编码 100710)
商 务 印 书 馆 发 行
北 京 冠 中 印 刷 厂 印 刷
ISBN 978 - 7 - 100-09899 - 1

2014 年 8 月第 1 版   开本 787×1092 1/32
2016 年 3 月北京第 2 次印刷   印张 5⅞ 插页 1
定价:21.00 元